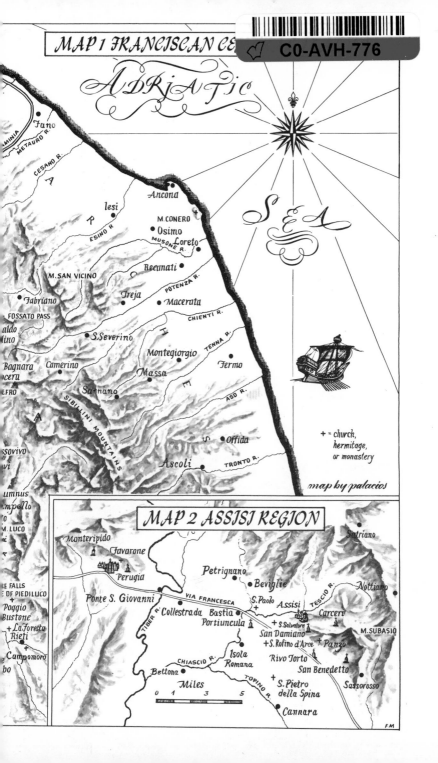

MAP 1 FRANCISCAN CE[...]

C0-AVH-776

ADRJATIC

SEA

Fano

METAURO R.

CESANO R.

A

Ancona

Iesi

M.CONERO

ESINO R.

Osimo

Loreto

MUSONE R.

Recanati

M.SAN VICINO

Treja

POTENZA R.

Fabriano

Macerata

FOSSATO PASS

CHIENTI R.

aldo
ino

S.Severino

Bagnara
ceru

Camerino

Montegiorgio

TENNA R.

Fermo

Massa

EFRO

Sarnano

ASO R.

SIBILLINI MOUNTAINS

ssovivo
vi

Offida

umnus
mpello
o
M.LUCO

Ascoli

TRONTO R.

+ = church,
hermitage,
or monastery

map by palacios

MAP 2 ASSISI REGION

Monteripido

Satriano

Favarone

Petrignano

Beviglie

Perugia

Nottiano

TESCIO R.

RE FALLS
DF PIEDILUCO
+
Poggio
Bustone
+ LaForesta
Rieti
+

VIA FRANCESCA

S.Paolo

Assisi

Ponte S. Giovanni

Carceri

TIBER R.

Collestrada

Bastia

San Damiano

+ S.Salvatore

M.SUBASIO

Portiuncula

+ S. Rofino d'Arce

Panzo

Campomoro
bo

Isola
Romana

Rivo Torto

San Benedetto

CHIASCIO R.

Bettona

Miles

0   1   3   5

TOPINO R.

+ S. Pietro
della Spina

Sassorosso

Cannara

FM

Commemorating the 800th Anniversary of the Birth of St. Francis 1182–1982

THE ROOTS OF ST. FRANCIS

A Popular History of the Church in Assisi and Umbria Before St. Francis
As Related to His Life and Spirituality

by
Raphael Brown
Secular Franciscan
Affiliate, O.F.M.

FRANCISCAN HERALD PRESS
Publishers of Franciscan Literature
Chicago Illinois 60609

Copyright © 1982
FRANCISCAN HERALD PRESS

Library of Congress Cataloging in Publication Data

Brown, Raphael, 1912-
  The roots of St. Francis.

  Bibliography: p.
  Includes index.
  1. Catholic Church—Italy—Assisi—History.
2. Catholic Church—Italy—Umbria—History. 3. Francis,
of Assisi, Saint, 1182–1226. 4. Assisi (Italy)—Church
history. 5. Umbria (Italy)—Church history. I. Title.
BX1548.A87B76   282'.45651   81-9724
ISBN 0-8199-0824-X   AACR2

Published with Ecclesiastical Permission
MADE IN THE UNITED STATES OF AMERICA

iv

The Author gratefully dedicates this book to these writers on Assisi and Umbria whose works have been indispensable in its preparation, and to the officers, scholars, librarians, editors, and publishers of the following historical institutions of Assisi and Umbria for their equally valuable publications and collections which preserve and transmit the living spiritual treasures of the beloved and blessed town and region of St. Francis:

St. Peter Damian   Mons. Michele Faloci Pulignani
Antonio Cristofani   Arnaldo Fortini
Mons. Ansano Fabbi   Mons. Aldo Brunacci
Padre Agostino Gemelli   Ugo Tarchi
Sir William Richmond   Michael Adams
Marcel Brion   Maurice Rowdon

Deputazione di Storia Patria per l'Umbria, Perugia
Università degli Studi di Perugia, Facoltà di Lettere e
    di Filosofia, Perugia; and its Centro di Studi Umbri,
    Gubbio
Accademia Spoletina—Centro Italiano di Studi
    sull'Alto Medioevo, Spoleto
Accademia Tudertina—Centro di Studi sulla
    Spiritualità Medievale, Todi
Accademia Properziana del Subasio, Assisi
Società Internazionale di Studi Francescani, Assisi

And especially, as all my books, to my valiant wife
    Gertrude.

v

Other Franciscan Books
by Raphael Brown

Our Lady and St. Francis
Fifty Animal Stories of St. Francis
The Wounded Heart: St. Charles of Sezze, Franciscan Brother
Franciscan Mystic, the Life of Blessed Brother Giles of Assisi
True Joy from Assisi: The Assisi Experience of Inner Peace and Joy. An Introduction to the Contemplative Spirituality of St. Francis

Translations

The Little Flowers of St. Francis
The Perfect Joy of St. Francis by Felix Timmermans
The Revelations of St. Margaret of Cortona by Ange Marie Hiral, O.F.M.
An Apostle of Two Worlds, Good Father Frederic Janssoone, O.F.M. by Romain Légaré, O.F.M.

Co-editor with Ignatius Brady, O.F.M., author of Introduction and Appendices, and compiler of Bibliography of *Saint Francis of Assisi, a Biography* by Omer Englebert, 2nd English ed., revised and augmented, and translated by Eve Marie Cooper

Acknowledgments

Grateful acknowledgment for permission to use quotations from the works listed below is hereby made to the following publishers:

Franciscan Friars of California, Simon Scanlon, O.F.M., editor, *Way of St. Francis* (San Francisco) June 1975: "Was St. Francis a 'Nature Mystic'?"

St. Anthony Messenger Press, Cincinnati: *Francis, The Journey and the Dream,* by Murray Bodo, O.F.M.

Macmillan, London and Basingstoke: *Assisi, Impressions of Half a Century,* by Sir William Richmond.

Vita e Pensiero, Milan: "Le fonti del Clitunno, paesaggio francescano," *Vita e Pensiero* 28 (1937) 227–30.

Penguin Books, Ltd., London: *The Letters of Pliny the Younger.*

Arthaud, Paris: *L'Ombrie,* by Marcel Brion.

While revising the page proofs of this book, I received an advance copy of an excellent review of its galleys written for the March 1982 issue of *The Cord.* I wish herewith to thank the reviewer, medievalist Dr. William R. Cook, for his sympathetic scholarly appraisal, and to acknowledge his correcting my error in identifying the Carolingian-era historian Paul the Deacon as a Byzantine rather than a Lombard. That correction has therefore been made in the printed text.

Contents

Foreword

by
Father David Temple, O.F.M.
Guardian, Mission Santa Barbara
Founder of its Center for Franciscan Resources
Provincial, Saint Barbara Province, 1952–1961

As we celebrate the 800th Anniversary of the Birth of St. Francis, the son of Pietro di Bernardone, we need to know about the roots of St. Francis.

This book is what we have needed for so many years. It will be a great aid in celebrating the Anniversary in a meaningful manner.

Our Saint's "roots" would seem to be a simple enough matter. Francis was born of a merchant father. He grew up in a city state that was struggling out of the feudal age. He lived in an Italy that bristled with spears even as it dreamed of peace. He loved the mode and manner of the troubadours and he took up their songs. Like his age, he was sometimes warrior and sometimes poet.

These are the roots of St. Francis as we know them. But they are not all. Raphael Brown in this book traces out the roots in long line, in depth, far back, almost two thousand years back into the history of the land of St. Francis.

As we advance with him page by page, we feel that we must know those roots in order to know Francis better. We must know those strong roots which make tough and tenacious purchase in hard rock. We must appreciate better the tenuous hair-roots which carry life in the world of the spirit.

This is not a history of Assisi. Rather it is an account of persons and places and a recalling of tides and of times which were roots in the life and spirituality of St. Francis of Assisi.

In this cavalcade through the ages in Umbria we encounter such personages as Hannibal, the poet Propertius, King Totila the Goth, St. Gregory the Great, Charlemagne, St. Peter Damian—and among related modern figures Goethe and Carducci and Padre Gemelli. And we see parts of the Umbrian scene as described by writers like Pliny the Younger, Lord Byron, Nathaniel Hawthorne, Georges Goyau, Edward Hutton, and Ernest Raymond.

These roots of the Poverello are many, and we have never had them placed before us in such full coverage, at least not in English—or in any language as far as I am aware. We are therefore grateful to the author that at this Anniversary we have a root system that seems substantially complete.

As we celebrate the Anniversary, we will hold conferences. We will have exhibitions of pictures. We will publish texts and studies. Above all we will strive to sharpen ourselves to respond more effectively to the ever keen challenge of Francis' call. We will do this better if we are conscious of his roots, hence of ours too.

St. Francis, as he comes forth from these pages, walks in the spirit as he has always walked, but we see him, even as he is about to strike out on new trails, along ways that have been grooved by many feet. Of course, he will do surprising things, but the stage setting for the surprises is more clearly seen. We see here the backdrop for that Francis who was always electric in response to the inspiration at the instant of its flash. We think that we understand him better in his homeland as he follows Umbri, Romans, martyrs, bishops, feudal lords, and contemplatives, because among these we find his roots.

We are particularly grateful for the introduction into the

Umbrian world. We have been long assured that there are massive Umbrian building stones in Assisi, fitted together by masons
who took pride in their craft. They endure as foundations of
parts of the city wall, and some still form the solid support of
some of the houses.

But the Umbrian in St. Francis does not end with the stones. It
is in his blood. There is in him that swift moving of the soul that
prays well on the Umbrian mountain. There is something in him
that sings on the Umbrian plain. In a flow that is subtle and sure
this enters his spirituality. It is an Umbrian man who sees God. It
is an Umbrian who surrenders totally to the Gospel.

There were bishops in St. Francis' life and there are bishops in
this book. They built and they rebuilt the church in Assisi. We
have heard their names but they have been moving in a background which we could not penetrate, even though we stood on
tip-toes and peered with all our might. The bishops are important because, when at the renunciation Bishop Guido put his
cloak about Francis, he is standing for all the bishops of Assisi.
He is doing what each of them wished to do: to put his mantle
about a man who was making himself so poor that he could
stand on the bare truth of the Gospel. The cloak of Bishops
Guglielmo and Ugo has finally found the man who will rebuild
the church of Assisi.

We have need of the account of the martyrs of Assisi who fell
under the sword that first came down heavy at Rome and then in
the outlying municipalities. We have long heard about the martyrs because they occupy a prominent place in the devotion of
Assisi. We have paused at the tomb of St. Victorinus in the
Benedictine church of San Pietro. We have stood with large
wonder before the sarcophagus of St. Rufinus in his cathedral.
We have reflected at the memorial chapel of St. Felicianus as we
descended to San Damiano. We have picked up their history in
bits and patches, and these did not always fit together. What we
have needed is the sharp knife which would separate legend
from founded tradition because there has always been a vivid

remembering of these three in the spiritual consciousness of Assisi. They were not far away when Francis set out on the mission to Morocco and they were very near him when in Egypt he insisted on seeing the Sultan so that he might immediately urge him to be baptized.

The reader will find many surprises in these pages. The roots of St. Francis reach out into unsuspected areas. Monte Luco and the Clitunno will be a surprise for many as they are set into the Franciscan picture.

The pounding march of Hannibal's armies might not seem to have much to do with the coming of Francis, until we survey the ground and fit together the history. When he fasted on the island on Lake Trasimeno, he was intent on reconciliation and forgiveness and peace, but he never quite forgot that on the shoreline yonder Hannibal's troops had caved in the Roman with an ambush that catapulted into a complete rout.

Perhaps we had passed quickly over the Roman remains in Assisi, because, as we said, everyone comes here to mark out the footprints of St. Francis. But Francis admired the Minerva Temple and wondered at the firm work of the bridges and appreciated the design of a then "modern" house set solidly beside a Roman gate. All this was important to him because his city was forged by the welding of several cultures. While none of them remained completely, none of them had passed entirely.

From these surprises, and many more, there stands forth a richer Francis and perhaps a more surprising one. We know him better as we understand the tree better when we know the ground and site on which it stands.

From these pages St. Francis comes forth as a man of his age who went on to become a man of any age. Into the world of Francis there came voices. They were of the past, but they resounded in the present. There were saints who had gone to God, but some of the saint always remains. There were differences that had never been resolved, feuds that had never been settled.

There was the building of the house of God that had never been finished. There was the memory of men who stood like giants against the Umbrian sky. There was the need of men, and this great desire shook the church like a fever.

This was the world and this was the church of Francis. This was the world in which he had been shaped. This was the world which he was to shape. To know him truly it is necessary to see him in the midst of it and to know well his roots.

This study of the roots of St. Francis is a great help to us because we need to meet the real Francis. We want to see him whole—and if there is a trace of the brown earth, the umber of Umbria, on him, so much the better.

This Francis stands on the shoulders of those who built Assisi's past. The roots make clear to us not only the point from which he started but also, in some measure, the manner in which he moved forward.

A return to roots can be nostalgic and it can be chastening. It can stir warm memories and it can challenge the soul. As we survey the grip and girth of the roots, we are moved with a kind of wonder which is not far from tears. We are in deep awe at the beginnings of St. Francis and we stand in even more profound reverence at his continuing growth in the world of the spirit. We are grateful for the magnificent growth and for the full flowering of the tree.

But in the vital surge of life like that of the Franciscan ideal there is also the sharp point of challenge. The tree wants to continue to grow and that depends on us.

We must not let the high prayer of St. Francis simply flutter like a leaf in the wind. We must not allow poverty to die on the vine. We can not permit the great desire to be poor little people to languish like a broken twig at the end of the branch.

Whether we are recalling Monte Luco or remembering Trasimeno we keep hearing the words of St. Francis: "What was mine to do I have done. May the Lord give you to do what is yours."

Introduction

Why in the world should anyone research and write—and why should you read—two books on Assisi before St. Francis, hence apparently without him, like Hamlet without Hamlet?

The reason is very simple: in order to know and to understand Francis better. To see him more clearly against the colorful backdrop of his beloved town and region and their living past. Above all in order to grasp how profoundly and powerfully St. Francis absorbed and transmitted the ever living, ever reviving mainstream tradition of Christian contemplative-active spirituality.

So these two books, *The Roots of St. Francis* and *Forefathers of St. Francis,* are not just a popular history of the church and saints of Assisi and Umbria during that church's first thousand years, roughly from A.D. 200 to 1200. And they are definitely *not* "Assisi without St. Francis." Rather they survey the dramatic growth of the church and evoke the spiritual giants of those ten centuries in that area in terms of and *as intimately related to the life and spirituality of St. Francis.* Direct or indirect links to him, to his actions or words or spirit reappear continuously and consistently; most are listed in the index under "Francis of Assisi." In one typical chapter, for example, they are found on two of every three pages. He is always either on the stage or in the wings of these two books.

My primary purpose in undertaking this project of explora-
tion in an almost totally unexplored field has been to throw new
light on the deeper meaning of those striking words so crucial in
the Saint's conversion, vocation, and spirituality, which he heard
the animated Christ say to him from the beautiful painted
wooden Crucifix of San Damiano:

"*Go, Francis, repair My house which, as you see, is completely destroyed.*"

Yes, "completely destroyed," *tota destruitur.* Not just, as usually
mistranslated: falling into ruin. No: destroyed, demolished. By
someone. By whom?

And what is the fuller sense of *domus mea?* Note well: My
"*house*" and not the usual mistranslation, My "church." Why was
"house" used rather than "church"? No doubt because "house"
could mean more than just the chapel and even more than the
Church as a whole. And because it could mean all three: the
dilapidated chapel of San Damiano outside Assisi; the entire
Roman Catholic Church throughout Europe; and third, as I
explained in *True Joy from Assisi* (TJA 159–160), the inner house
of the Christian soul where God wants to dwell.

For it is perfectly clear that we cannot "repair" the Church at
large unless we repair, remodel, renew, and remake our own
soul or inner house. As St. Francis often stressed to his followers
and wrote in his First Rule: "Let us always make in ourselves a
little dwelling and abode of Him who is the Lord God Almighty,
Father and Son and Holy Spirit" (1R 22; see TJA 161).

But beyond and collateral to that inward sense of the condition of Francis' still to be converted soul at that moment in San
Damiano, to what extent and in what ways was the external
House of God, the Latin Church, in historical actuality "completely destroyed" around the year 1200, and not so much generally throughout Christendom but specifically in Assisi and
Umbria? What light does its evolution during its first thousand
years in that particular region throw on the meaning of those
strange, startling, lapidary words, "completely destroyed"?

Furthermore, what light does the history of Assisi throw on those surprising words which Francis applied to its inhabitants in his Blessing of his hometown before he died: ". . . of old this city was, as I believe, a place and dwelling of evil and wicked men and was of evil fame in all these provinces" (CA 99. SP 124; see TJA 16-20).

We shall therefore explore and describe, in a popular presentation for the general public or at least for all serious students of St. Francis, the history and conditions of the church in Assisi and Umbria in this first book, *The Roots of St. Francis*, and in its sequel, *Forefathers of St. Francis*, the major saints, both the contemplative monks and hermits and the outstanding reformer bishops of Umbria.

I will await the end of that second book to evolve and formulate my maturing conclusions regarding the ultimate nature and significance of the "destruction" of the House of God in Assisi around the year 1205, when young Francesco di Pietro di Bernardone received his vocation to "repair" it.

This historical excursion is doubly timely just now. With the celebrations of the 800th Anniversary of his Birth in 1982, there will not be for another century such an opportune occasion to dig into the "roots" and state of the church in Assisi at the time of his birth. And with the widespread popularity and influence of Arthur Haley's book and television drama *Roots,* the current intense interest in tracing back family histories makes this study of the civic and spiritual roots of St. Francis uniquely timely and relevant.

However, it must be stressed that unfortunately the actual family roots or genealogy of Francis, son of Peter Bernardone, cannot be reliably documented, even by Assisi's and the Saint's great archival expert and historian Arnaldo Fortini, beyond Francis' grandfather Bernardone, of whom we know only that he too was a merchant (FNV II, 93, 100). Other ancestors' names—another Pietro and Bernardo?—remain conjectural, i.e., unprovable. On a recent Jewish ancestry theory, see Appendix C.

Therefore, we will be tracing the "roots" of St. Francis in the soil not of genealogy but of local history and specifically of church history and the history of spirituality, rather than political and social history, municipal or regional.

As remote, earliest "roots" or background, the four Chapters of the Prologue describe the pre-Christian culture in Umbria of the Etruscans, the Umbri, and the Romans. Then, in Chapters V–IX, we witness the arrival, preaching, and martyrdom of the first apostles of Christ in the region, notably St. Felician, Umbria's first great apostle-and-martyr, who also literally planted the cross in Assisi, near San Damiano. The testimony of the martyrs requires an essay on St. Francis' burning desire to die as a martyr.

Especially significant as a stepping-stone between the paganism of classical antiquity and the coming of Christianity in Umbria is an Interlude (Chap. IV) on the beautiful little park, springs, and temple of the Clitunno River near Spoleto, because this famous site evolved from the popular shrine of a Roman river-god into one of the first Christian churches and baptismal centers of Umbria. Notable reactions to the "Franciscan" charm of the site by two modern Italian writers, the poet Giosuè Carducci and Franciscan Father Agostino Gemelli, are quoted.

In Part Two (Chaps. X–XV) the dire tribulations of the church in Umbria during the Dark Ages of the years 400–1000 are outlined: the invasions and occupations by the Goths and Lombards, the latter as Arians persecuting the Catholics, with efforts at pacification under Pope St. Gregory the Great and the Emperor Charlemagne, culminating in the potentially apocalyptic turning-point of the year 1000.

Part Three (Chapters XVI–XXI) covers the dramatic conflicts

that divided the people and church of Assisi during the eleventh and twelfth centuries, when the rising mercantile bourgeoisie challenged and broke the power of the feudal aristocracy, and the church developed two cathedrals, with the priors and canons of the new Duomo of San Rufino contesting the authority of the bishops in Santa Maria.

This significant struggle reached a climax in 1198, when young Francis probably took part in the sacking of La Rocca, the feudal fortress dominating the town, after which some noble families (including that of the future St. Clare) sought refuge as exiles in Perugia. That victory of the middle classes of the now dominant *comune* (city-state), personified by Francis' rich merchant father, assumed a symbolic triumph in the completion of the handsome Romanesque façade of San Rufino during the lifetime of St. Francis.

Having quoted in Chapter III on Roman Assisi the best extant description of the classical Temple of Minerva on the Piazza, written by the famous German poet and philosopher Goethe, we add an Appendix A on his little-known but noteworthy visit to Assisi in 1786 and on his surprising attitude then and later toward St. Francis.

Appendix B deals with the Saint's Christian nature-mysticism.

Appendix D lists more "Needed Studies."

Whereas *The Roots of St. Francis* treats of events and trends affecting the church in Assisi and Umbria in its first thousand years, *Forefathers of St. Francis* will concentrate on five major personalities who strove to "repair" God's House there in a spiritual way—and succeeded—during the eleventh and twelfth centuries. Four were great contemplatives who were also active as reformers: Saints Romuald, founder of the Hermits of Camaldoli; Peter Damian, hermit and cardinal; Bonfil, Bishop of Foligno; and Ubaldo, Bishop of Gubbio. The fifth is the fas-

cinating and brilliant, but as yet almost unknown Bishop of Assisi
in 1179, Rufinus II or Magister Rufinus, author of a remarkable
pre-Franciscan treatise "On the Good of Peace," a digest of
which will be included.

Forefathers will also sketch the significant parallels between the
spirituality of St. Francis and that of St. Gregory the Great, "the
Father of the Middle Ages," and that of the twelfth century.
Those similarities will demonstrate how the "roots" of St. Francis
were irrigated by the mainstream currents of the Latin
contemplative-active or mixed life tradition. For it will become
apparent that those spiritual forefathers lived and taught a pattern of contemplative prayer and active evangelization which
forms the historic background of the active-contemplative "mix"
of St. Francis that I outlined in *True Joy from Assisi* (TJA 179–
184). As a relevant case-study in pre-Franciscan Italian eremit-
ical spirituality, *Forefathers* will include an Appendix on St.
Romuald's powerful yet almost unknown "Brief Rule for Hermit
Novices."

Apart from lists of bishops and a few short articles in encyclo-
pedias, I have not found a history or study of the church in
Assisi—a truly amazing situation! Antonio Cristofani's still useful history of the town and the works of Arnaldo Fortini treat
the church only incidentally. In English we have only very brief
sketches of general history in the books on Assisi by Lina Duff-
Gordon and Clarissa Goff. The otherwise excellent *Forerunners
of St. Francis* by Ellen Scott Davison (London and New York,
1928) deals with the broad Italian and European scene and not
with Umbria. Even the splendid recent studies of conditions in
Assisi and Umbria around 1200 of the annual meetings of the
thriving revived International Society of Franciscan Studies and
the new Center of Umbrian Studies, alas, have not (yet) treated
the church in Assisi, apart from one announced lecture which
was not delivered or published.

The most puzzling and deplorable lacuna is the overlong absence of one or more comprehensive studies of Assisi's great yet unknown, though well documented, Bishop Rufinus II, its most important bishop both on his own rich merits and because he flourished there around the time when Francis was born. Now it appears that such studies of his life and writings may at last soon be forthcoming, thanks to the initiative of the Diocesan Archivist Monsignor Aldo Brunacci.

These two books have therefore been produced as pioneering surveys of a relatively unexplored subject by an amateur popularizer in a distant land laboring without adequate studies by scholars. This handicap may account for some—though not all—of their faults.

The Bibliography and Abbreviations include important books, articles, and reference works which proved indispensable and will be useful to students. They are arranged by subject sections covering several related chapters.

Certainly the colorful history of the church in Umbria and Assisi before St. Francis merits far more attention than it has had so far, not only because it produced one of the greatest of the many Saints of Italy or of the Catholic Church as a whole, but above all because the House of God in that region has been the blessed soil and fertile garden of that universally recognized and admired phenomenon known as Umbrian mysticism, with its Franciscan keynote of contemplation and prayer as well-springs of compassionate action. And that is a phenomenon of first rank importance in the religious history of mankind.

Abundant concrete evidence of the spiritual fruitfulness of Umbria is to be seen today in its handsome cathedrals and imposing monasteries (even their ruins), and in its many strikingly simple and beautiful, i.e., "Franciscan," Romanesque churches and chapels, as also in the lovely scenic sites of those isolated hillside hermitages which were re-occupied or founded by Francis and his friars.

Thus the famous *Umbria verde* merged into *Umbria monastica-*

eremitica which in turn became *Umbria serafica-francescana,* all together forming *Umbria santa, Umbria mistica.*

Therefore we who aspire to follow—as far as we can—in the footsteps of St. Francis, whether in his Umbria or wherever Providence has placed us to live and spread his spirit and message, must do what he told Blessed Angela of Foligno to do: ". . . love what I myself loved" (see TJA xxxix). Surely he had a very special love for his province and its "lovely Valley of Spoleto" and for all of his hometown, little Assisi, from the Portiuncola up to the Carceri on Mount Subasio (see TJA 14–20).

For that is where his "roots" were deeply entrenched, both in the land and in its still living past. And there his spiritual roots penetrated most deeply of all into the humus of that "destroyed" House of God, in those plain, simple Romanesque churches and chapels where he so often prayed and suffered and exulted, in the chapels of San Damiano and the Little Portion of St. Mary of the Angels, in the Duomo of Santa Maria and the new House of San Rufino, as in the churches of the neighboring towns of Perugia, Gubbio, Foligno, and Spoleto.

It has been wisely said that Christians are not to plunge their roots too deeply into the soil of this earth. And no doubt that is true insofar as by earth we mean this passing, sin-drenched, "worldly" world ruled by "the Prince of this world." Yet it is also a fact that Providence provides us with a set of roots in the site and culture and influences of the places where we are born and grow up and live. Surely "rootless" persons may seem to be free without thereby being sound or happy.

No doubt the Saints are those who relate to their "roots" most effectively. Without repudiating their origins, they succeed in outgrowing and detaching themselves from the bonds of all this-worldly attachments. They overcome and surpass and supernaturalize their native roots in this world, thereby acquiring undying new spiritual roots in that heavenly homeland, the

New Jerusalem of the Kingdom which descends daily into their souls in prayer (see TJA 197).

It is in this sense that we can best understand how St. Francis accepted and thrived on the spiritual roots which God gave him in the church, both of Assisi and of Rome, to both of which he ever remained so deeply loyal. It was because he drew rich nourishment from those roots that he was able radiantly to "repair" and restore and renew the temporarily "destroyed" House of God of his time, first in his own soul and then in countless other souls, first in Assisi and Umbria, then throughout the Western Church and now all over the world.

Certainly Jesus Christ, the Jesus of the Gospels, was his tap root. And it was by plunging into the deepest layer of that supreme Root that he brought forth new vitality in the church. No doubt an acute critic might claim that the spiritual roots of St. Francis as a deliberate imitator of Christ should be traced in Palestine rather than in Umbria. And that is partly correct, obviously, but it is not the whole story and hardly any of the actual historical background. As a matter of fact, in these two books as in *True Joy from Assisi,* we find some striking parallels (not links) between St. Francis and early Syrian spirituality, as well as a direct link between Syrian monasticism and Monte Luco (see II.5), and between early Christian art in Syria and in the Spoleto region (see IV.4. Also TJA xxxviii, 162, 178).

These two books will, I trust, demonstrate how deeply the spiritual roots of St. Francis plunge into the fertile soil of Umbria and how richly they were nourished there by the ever potent stream and currents of the great patristic-monastic tradition of Western Christian mixed contemplative-active spirituality.

Again I am happy to express my very cordial thanks to Father David Temple, O.F.M., for another beautiful and perceptive Foreword and for the use of his Center for Franciscan Resources at Old Mission, Santa Barbara. Also to Monsignor Aldo

Brunacci, Diocesan Archivist of Assisi; Father Salvator Butler, O.F.M., at San Damiano in Assisi; Father Herbert Palmer, O.S.B., librarian of St. Charles Priory, Oceanside; and Dr. Lydia von Auw, for loans of materials, as well as to the librarians of the Franciscan Institute at St. Bonaventure University.

The Roman dramatist Terence (d. 159 B.C.) left this keynote of all humanists: *Homo sum: humani nil a me alienum puto.* "I am a man. I consider nothing human alien to me."

May *The Roots of St. Francis* and *Forefathers of St. Francis* bring the Little Poor Man of Assisi into sharper focus for all who join the author in adapting that formula to read: We consider nothing about St. Francis alien to us, no, not even his spiritual roots and forefathers.

Vista, San Diego County
Southern California, U.S.A.
October 4, 1980
Feast of St. Francis
in the Preparatory Year before
the 800th Anniversary of his Birth

> HAPPY BIRTHDAY, DEAR FATHER FRANCIS!
> Thank you for drawing us through your joy
> and your true joy, merrily and Mary-ly,
> to know, love, and serve our Great King
> and Lord Jesus Christ.

Prologue

Umbria Before Christ
750 B.C.–A.D. 200

I

The Etruscans and the Umbri
Perugia versus Assisi

Again, why when focusing the historian's magic zoom lense back through time to produce an in-depth cinerama of the religious backdrop of the life and message of St. Francis, now in this 800th Anniversary of his Birth, why extend our telescopic vista still another two millenia into the murky past of Italy? Why try to trace his "roots" way back to the pre-Christian, even the pre-Roman civilization of the peoples known as the Etruscans and the Umbri who flourished in Central Italy and specifically in Perugia and Assisi even before the foundation of Rome?

1 The First Peoples of Umbria

One answer might be: simply because we can hardly regress further in time. I would certainly not suggest that there is any link connecting the Saint's biblical predilection for stones and rocks and caves with the Stone Age cavemen of Umbria. However, visitors to the grottoes of his companions at the Carceri Hermitage above Assisi cannot be blamed if they think of those hardy hermit-friars as early Franciscan "cavemen."

But a more valid reason for this Prologue on pre-Christian

Umbria is the claim of some modern writers that the medieval inhabitants of Umbria appear to have inherited several traits of psychology from their remote ancestors, the Etruscans and the Umbri.

Two relevant facts of history are beyond question: just as Perugia and Assisi fought a series of wars during the Middle Ages (in one of which young Francis enlisted, fought, and was captured), so the Etruscans and the Umbri lived for centuries in deep-seated hostility which was strikingly recorded before the year 200 B.C. by the Umbri in the bronze Tablets of Gubbio: "Destruction to all of the race of the Tuski, their magistrates in or out of office, their young warriors armed or not—may they be put to sudden flight, bite the dust, be drowned, beaten, defeated" (Fabbi 84).

It has been observed that such traits appear to come back to life in figures like Saints Benedict and Francis and the Umbrian warlords or *condottieri*. Thus many centuries later we find the inhabitants of Umbria displaying in their culture and history the ferocity and religiosity of the Etruscans, the piety and humility of the Umbri, and the achievements of the Romans in law and the art of governing.

Werner Keller and others have even noted Etruscan traits in the art and culture of the Renaissance in Tuscany (Etruria), for instance in Dante and Michelangelo.

These remotest "roots" are therefore relevant and must be briefly examined. In Section 4 below several tenuous links between St. Francis and the Etruscans and the Umbri will be mentioned.

Geographically, the Upper Tiber River separated the Etruscans from the Umbri, with the former to the west and the latter to the east of the river. The towns of Assisi, Gubbio, and Spoleto were Umbrian, while Perugia and Orvieto were major Etruscan centers (though included in modern Umbria).

2 The Enigmatic and Sophisticated Etruscans

The relatively sudden appearance around 750 B.C. in central Italy of the highly developed, sophisticated Etruscan civilization remains one of the major enigmas of history. Even today, with an explosion of archaeological discoveries and in-depth studies, the people and culture of ancient Etruria retain a double mystery: their origin and their language.

Ancient and modern historians cannot agree on whether the Etruscans were indigenous to Italy or came from the north or the east, and if the latter, from the Aegean or Asia Minor or Phoenicia. Their advanced civilization has been aptly described as like an oasis suddenly transplanted from the Near East to Italy.

However, their rise and decline, their primary role in the founding of Rome by the Etruscan King Tarquinius Priscus around the year 575 B.C. (not 753 as in later Roman legend), and their subjection by Rome in the third century B.C., are well documented. Several excellent popular introductory books are listed in the Bibliography.

It is indeed surprising to learn that during the brilliant Periclean Age in Greece (around 440 B.C.), a highly developed culture thrived in Central Italy and right in Perugia, within sight of Assisi. For the civilization of the Etruscans was one of affluence and luxury, with an economy based on flourishing agriculture, mining, and overseas trade. The Etruscan genius proved especially inventive in urban planning, with paved and drained streets meeting at right angles, and in irrigation and land reclamation by networks of canals and tunnels. Their skilled crafts included ornate pottery and delicate goldsmith and metal work, as well as painting and sculpture, often influenced by Greek models.

The character and psychology of the Etruscans have been

described as active, energetic, creative, exuberant, urbane, charming, extravagant, high-spirited, with a passion for the good life, hedonistic, and sensual. Their women lived a freer life style than the Romans, using eye and lip make-up and blond bleaches. Dentistry even provided crowns and dentures.

The Etruscans were known in antiquity for their intensive religiosity taking the form of an obsessive preoccupation with discerning the will of the gods that governed all events. For them, an occurence did not have meaning because it happened, but it occurred in order to convey a meaning. Hence their elaborate cult of soothsaying and augury by divination: interpreting omens in lightning, bird flights, and animal livers. It was an Etruscan augur who warned Caesar: "Beware of the ides of March!" They had a profound conviction of the mystic unity of cosmos and microcosm, of heaven, earth, and underworld, and hence of life here and beyond.

Believing that ancestors inhabited their tombs or necropolises (cities of the dead), the Etruscans built enormous, well-planned cemeteries, often vaster than nearby towns, with streets of chamber mausoleums stocked with domestic utensils and belongings of the deceased and decorated with colorful paintings of banquet or hunting scenes and with ornate sculptured sarcophagi and reclining statues of the dead ancestors, often serenely smiling an "enduring smile."

But as the augurs correctly foretold, with the rise of Rome Etruria was doomed to decline, and its late art took on a somber, gloomy, mournful aspect, the former joy yielding to an eruption of hideous demons and hellish chimera and griffins. Incidently, the mythical griffin (half-lion, half-eagle), imported from Near Eastern art and religion, became the municipal symbol of Perugia in the Middle Ages.

Astride its five hill-spurs on Assisi's western horizon, Perugia was for centuries a leading center of Etruscan civilization, being one of the twelve major city-states that joined in a federation too loose to resist the inexorable expansion of Roman military power. It was also famed for the skill of its craftsmen working in bronze.

At the foot of an eastern spur, within a mile of Ponte San Giovanni and the Tiber where young Francis and the troops of Assisi were defeated, lies the massive underground necropolis of the wealthy Volumnii family, dating from the second century B.C., which is well worth a visit. The collection of Etruscan art in Perugia's Civic Museum in the former San Domenico Friary is one of the richest in Italy (described in detail in Rowdon 65–70, 79–84).

South of Perugia, Todi and Orvieto have notable Etruscan remains. The latter was a major religious center, attracting pilgrims to the annual festivals at nearby Vulsinii from much of Umbria as late as the fourth century A.D.

3 The Humble and Pious Umbri

Relatively little is known about the origin and culture of the Umbri, an Italic people who settled on the east of the Upper Tiber. In the third century B.C. they submitted to Roman rule and influences. Their simpler, more rustic civilization, without tombs rich in archaeological remains, was less urbane and sophisticated than that of their Etruscan neighbors across the Tiber; even today the people of Assisi and Gubbio are not so cosmopolitan as the Perugians.

However, considerable light is thrown on the religion and society of the Umbri around the year 200 B.C. by Gubbio's important Iguvine Tablets, seven bronze plates discovered there in 1444, now on display in the museum. The largest measure about one by two feet, with clear script engraved on both sides. The language is ancient Umbrian, now deciphered (unlike Etruscan), but the letters are Latin and Etruscan, reading from right to left, with reversed E and N. The text deals with the rituals and rules of a religious fraternity known as the Atiedi (full analysis in Fabbi 78–87).

The Tablets provide significant information about the culture of the Umbri. Their towns were organized as city-states having an acropolis (sacred hill with temple), a square urban area, and three sacred gates in the city walls. Citizens of the leading families formed a civic assembly ruled by elders or magistrates.

The priests of the Atiedi presided over ceremonial sacrifices and divinations. The rites included sacred dances, offerings of oxen or goats to the gods (many corresponding to Roman dieties such as Jupiter and Mars); also various prayers for the protection and prosperity of the community, some of which ring with a hieratic solemnity: "To you, divine Jupiter, be sacred the city of Gubbio. May its magistrates, priests, citizens, cattle, harvests be protected. Surround the sacred temple, the city, and its people with your protection. May your protecting peace descend over the city of Gubbio and its people."

A foremost modern historian of Umbria, Monsignor Ansano Fabbi, comments that "when we speak of 'mystical Umbria' it is right to go beyond the Middle Ages, back to the fervent prayers of Gubbio as inspired by the soul of the ancient Umbri" (Fabbi 80, 83).

4 *St. Francis and the Etruscans and Umbri*

Perhaps the most striking parallel between St. Francis and his Order of Minor Brothers and the early Umbrians is that pre-Christian religious brotherhood whose "rule" is recorded in the Tablets of Gubbio.

While it is true that the ancient enmity between Perugia and

Assisi can be traced back to the Etruscans and the Umbri a millenium earlier, yet there is no record of major battles between them then. In fact, despite their ethnic differences and underlying antagonism, the two peoples, as well as the early Romans, actually shared a religious culture that compenetrated their society. Thus Umbria in those times has been well described as "really a marriage between the Umbri and the Etruscans, combining a certain light intimacy with something mystical and sad" (Rowdon 12).

It is not hard to discern here some of the traits in the personality and spirit of St. Francis, the would-be warrior who evolved into a great mystic with "a certain light intimacy."

An enlightening study could and should be made of his relations with the people of Perugia, his outspoken condemnation of their warring knights (2C 37), and his spiritual conquest of many souls among them. A local proverb holds that "the people of Perugia are either angels or demons." Observers point to the "angelic" sweetness and gentleness of the Umbrian school of painters, in sharp contrast with the "demonic" savagery of Perugia's civil wars and tyrants. However, they also stress a striking Franciscan harmony achieved by modern Perugians which radiates an almost mystical calm and serenity, an attractive grace and charm and amiability, a smiling tolerance and gentility. Who can say or measure to what extent those traits are due to an Etruscan inheritance or to a Christian and Franciscan influence or both?

So too who can explain those elements in the psychology of the modern Umbrians which seem so remarkably "Franciscan"? Their nature has been termed simple, rustic, sturdy, vigorous, humble, cheerful, kindly, gentle, pious, mystical, and happy.

It is noteworthy that St. Francis seems to have evangelized the territory of the Umbri east of the Tiber more than that of ancient Etruria. Apart from Perugia and Cortona, we have relatively few accounts of his visits to the former Etruscan cities of

Todi and Orvieto and the villages of that region. However, three of his twenty hermitages were located in Etruria: those of Sarteano, Cetona, and the Celle of Cortona.

Of course he often saw in Assisi, Perugia, Spello, and elsewhere the massive city walls built by the Umbri or Etruscans, consisting of heavy blocks of travertine (Tiber stone) perfectly fitted together, and he must have seen the Etruscan cemeteries above ground, though not the forgotten underground tomb chambers.

In this connection—if there is any—the Etruscans shared a belief with the Greeks that birds often manifested sympathy at the death of human beings, and this reminds us of the joyful singing of the larks above the Portiuncola during the death of St. Francis, who had a special affection for larks and often urged them to praise the Lord (3C 32. CA 110. B 14.6).

So too the belief of the Etruscans that the dead continued to hover around their tombs and that their surviving friends could commune with them there reminds us of the vibrant, living, radiating presence of the Saint in Assisi today which visitors have reported is especially perceptible at his Tomb (see TJA 28, 72).

Incidentally, a striking (non-Franciscan) survival of Etruscan customs relating to the dead is the traditional tap of a hammer on the head of a just deceased pope.

Finally, it is a ludicrous irony of nonhistory and a minor embarassment to Franciscans that in the absence of authentic information about the early history of Perugia two sons of St. Francis, among others, fabricated fantastic legends claiming that the city was founded either by some companions of Ulysses or even by Noah himself. Those two imaginative friars were Fra Bonifazio of Verona, author of the *Eulistea,* a chronicle of Perugia down to 1293 of real value for his own times, the thirteenth century, for instance for the battle with Assisi in 1202; and Fra Felice Ciatti whose history of Perugia appearing in 1638 has been called "a marvel of misdirected erudition."

II

Roman Umbria

1 *Was St. Francis "Roman"?*

Was St. Francis "Roman"? And if so, in what sense? And to what extent?

We know that he was a deliberately steadfast Roman Catholic, an outstandingly loyal follower of that Galilean fisherman turned fisher of souls named Peter who evangelized Rome and died there. Francis had a special devotion to St. Peter, which has not yet been studied in depth as it merits.

But we are concerned here with the question: To what extent and in what way or ways was Francis a more or less conscious heir of the deep-flowing Roman ideals and ethos which were absorbed and transmitted by the peoples of Central Italy like the Umbrians?

Rome ruled Umbria for over seven centuries, from about 300 B.C. until the barbarian invasions around A.D. 400. Then the successors of St. Peter, directly and through their bishops, the successors of the Apostles, found themselves obliged by default to govern the area as far as eventually allowed by the rising power of the Lombard kings and the Frankish and then German emperors.

As we have seen, those great Umbrian figures, Saints Benedict and Francis, embodied several traits of character which were typical of their Etruscan, Umbrian, and Roman ancestors. It is noteworthy that both of them managed to combine discipline with militancy and sanctity. Most of all, they inherited a Roman sense of order and measure.

Both saints also reflect some of the basic elements of what I described in *True Joy from Assisi* (TJA 179–184) as "the St. Francis mix," namely a combination of action and contemplation, prayer and work, praise and service. Also a striking down-to-earth practicality and ability to judge and deal with different personalities. Both Saints were mystics, and both were founders and leaders of major movements. Both were innovators, yet also deeply conservative.

It would indeed be worthwhile for some scholar to make a thorough study of the survival of Etruscan, Umbrian, and Roman qualities in the psychological makeup of those two great Umbrian figures. Such a task is far beyond my ability, but I believe that it would document the survival of several traits of those cultures, especially the Roman. So perhaps, with all due reservations and caution, some of the spiritual "roots" of St. Francis may be traced back to various elements in the psychological pattern of the ancient Romans.

For instance, among a list of those traits compiled by one historian, the following seem to be relevant to the personality of St. Francis: preoccupation with the practical ethics of daily life, action rather than theory, adaptability, a combination of severity and tolerance, and most of all these three fundamental Roman virtues: *virtus,* courage and integrity; *gravitas,* earnestness; and *pietas,* duty toward God and society.

While the Poverello of Assisi may have lacked the Roman passion for law and order, it was one of the greatest strokes of his genius and wisdom that he willingly submitted and subjected himself and his Order to that Roman authoritarian structure surviving in the Roman Church. And he certainly had a good share of Roman practicality and preoccupation with the ethics of daily life, especially in view of the fact that he was such a contemplative mystic.

Apart from studies of his sojourns in Rome and his relations with the popes and curia cardinals (see EBB 584), I have found only two brief essays on his possible inheritance from ancient Rome, those by Chioccioni and Pierotti. Though they tend to blur Roman-ness with Roman Catholicism, yet they are right in stressing that the Saint did manifest a "Roman" universality in his mission to all men and a kind of *pax romana-franciscana* in his peacemaking.

No doubt St. Francis did not make a cult of the classic-papal ideal of a new Christian Roman empire, as did Dante, who almost made of Rome an Italian New Jerusalem. Yet Francis surely shared the poet's lofty aspiration to "be forever a citizen of that Rome where Christ is Roman," i.e., Heaven (*Purgatorio* 32.101–102).

In any case, because Umbria and Assisi and all of Franciscan Italy were colonized and ruled and deeply influenced by Roman civilization for over seven centuries, a book on the spiritual roots of St. Francis must include chapters on Roman Umbria and Roman Assisi, with special attention to those enduring remnants of ancient Rome which he saw around him and which form an essential part of the backdrop of his daily life in his native town and region.

2 Umbria under Rome

Umbria is still rich today in Roman monuments and remains. They include bridges at Narni, Foligno, and Spoleto; amphitheaters at Gubbio, Terni, and Spoleto; massive city walls at Spello and Perugia; and temples at Assisi, Bevagna, and Spoleto.

Is it a mere coincidence that both of Assisi's most famous sons were important poets: St. Francis, of course, and the Augustan era elegiac poet Sextus Propertius (see III.1). Among other distinguished men born in Umbria or of Umbrian parentage in Roman times were the historian Tacitus, born probably in Terni about A.D. 55, and the Emperor Vespasian, born in Rieti about A.D. 9, whose mother was from Nursia (now Norcia), the birthplace of St. Benedict and his sister, St. Scholastica. The popular dramatist Plautus (d. 184 B.C.) came from the mountains near La Verna in Tuscany. The writer Pliny the Younger (d. about A.D. 113) had a large country estate in the Upper Tiber Valley north of Città di Castello (then named Tifernum).

Rightly called "the Pompei of Umbria," the ruins of the Roman town of Carsulae between Terni and Todi are noteworthy for two reasons: the scenic beauty of the site amid rich meadows and gently sloping woodlands, praised by Tacitus and Pliny Junior; and the abundance of its recently excavated remains of temples, baths, fountains, a vast amphitheater and large theater, forum and law court, plus a lofty and majestic north gate-arch that Maurice Rowdon calls "one of the most inexplicably grand and unexpected sights we shall ever have."

Another British author, Beryl de Selincourt, has left us this perceptive evocation of Carsulae and St. Francis on p. 180 of her valuable *Homes of the First Franciscans:*

> One glorious relic of its past remains in the triumphal arch, which in lonely and solemn splendor towers above the country-side, pronouncing the dirge of the proud and ancient city.... Conspicuous for miles around, this solemn arch has power to cast a spell.... The generations which have passed since it stood a landmark to Francis on his way to that Rome of the Caesars of which it was once a symbol, seem gathered into the shadow of its age, as one generation: the distance of ages is bridged, and we stand on common ground with him, perhaps nearer in spirit than he to the great Roman world. We do not know what power it had to stir him after the current of his

early enthusiasm was turned; but the noble Roman relics with which he was surrounded in his native town must have given shape to some of those first dreams of glory.

St. Francis often passed by the ruins of Carsulae when he visited his hermitage known as L'Eremita di Cesi located on a hillside a steep hour's climb above Carsulae.

3 The Via Flaminia, Umbria's Roman Superhighway

In 295 B.C. an army of the expanding Roman Republic won a decisive victory over allied Etruscan and Umbrian forces at Sentino near Sassoferrato, marking the beginning of centuries of tolerant yet firm Roman rule over Umbria.

Around 220 Rome consolidated its dominion by building the famous Via Flaminia, a military highway extending northward through Umbria to link the capital with Ravenna on the Adriatic and thence with the plain of the Po and northern Italy by the Via Emilia running in a straight line from Rimini on the coast through Bologna to Milan.

For the next thousand years the Flaminia remained the principal eastern highway between Rome and northern Italy, as was on the west the Via Cassia through Tuscan Viterbo, Siena, and Lucca.

In Umbria the Flaminia originally went from Narni to Foligno through Carsulae and Bevagna, but by A.D 300 a branch through Terni and Spoleto superseded that route. In the sixth century another branch took on strategic value when Perugia became the main communications center of the Byzantine Exarchate between Rome and Ravenna (and Constantinople); it ran from Narni through Todi to Perugia and from there through Gubbio to Cagli and on the Flaminia.

We should note that placid little Assisi was not on any of these highways, as it lies half way between Foligno and Perugia.

The broad, uneven flagstones of the Via Flaminia, deeply grooved by chariot wheels and now overgrown with grass, can still be clearly seen at Carsulae, which served as an important traffic stopover between Narni and Foligno.

By the way, Carsulae also had an early Christian church dedicated to the popular Syrian physician Saints Cosmas and Damian, like Assisi's San Damiano.

4 *Hannibal Invades Umbria*

Assisi was so blessed with placid peace that not a single major event is recorded in its annals throughout the long era of the Roman Republic and Empire, though Umbria was the scene of two wars.

In 217 B.C., Hannibal, the shrewd thirty-year-old general from Carthage in North Africa, reached Lake Trasimene west of Perugia in his ambitious advance against Rome, after crossing the Alps with 40,000 infantry and cavalry troops—and one surviving elephant. Following him into Umbria were 20,000 Roman soldiers under the rash Consul Caius Flaminius.

During the night of June 23, Hannibal's main forces hid in the woods and hills along the lake's northern shore, while a decoy regiment went on toward Perugia. The incredibly careless Romans then proceeded along the shore, where they were in a position which the historian Livy termed "formed by nature for an ambush."

The Carthaginians attacked at dawn through a low mist and drove the dismayed Romans into the rushes and water, killing 15,000 men, including their leader. Three local place-names—Sanguineto, Ossaia, and Sepoltaia—gruesomely recall the blood, bones, and burying resulting from this slaughter.

Fourteen centuries later a young former soldier from Assisi fought a nonviolent battle of the spirit during a forty-day Lenten fast on an island in that lake, and won a lifelong victory of soul over body in deliberate imitation of his leader, Jesus Christ. As Ernest Raymond so aptly wrote of his visit to Trasimene: "I saw another figure moving along that road by the rushes: a simple figure in a homespun habit and cord. It was another conqueror of Italy." Later another of St. Francis' hermitage-friaries was founded on that island.

Hannibal, after his great victory, expected the Umbrians as a non-Roman people to side with him, but they did not. In fact he suffered a sharp repulse at Spoleto, before his second defeat of the Romans at Cannae in the south in 216 B.C. While marching from Trasimene to Spoleto his army must have passed along the plain below the walls of Assisi, evidently without bothering to besiege it.

The decision of the Umbrians to fight with the Romans against the invader in this Second Punic War shows that they accepted Roman rule, probably because Rome wisely allowed them to keep their local customs, government, and coinage, requiring only that they cooperate with Roman foreign policy by contributing troops for Rome's wars. It is known that Gubbio's soldiers fought effectively against Hannibal, and that Spoleto's stubborn resistance earned for it Rome's enduring gratitude and favor.

5 Monte Luco's Sacred Forest, Beloved by Michelangelo and St. Francis

The wooded hump of Monte Luco (or Monteluco) above Spoleto provides a significant example of Roman toleration of local Umbrian customs—as well as one of the two most beautiful

sites in St. Francis' beloved and lovely Valley of Spoleto. Both
were famed in classical antiquity. Both were well known to
him. And both remain as beautiful today as they were in the
thirteenth century and in ancient times. They are the sacred
forest on Monte Luco and the springs of the Clitunno River five
miles north of Spoleto; the latter will be fully treated in Chapter IV.

From the point of view of religious history Monte Luco is
probably the most important spiritual center in Umbria, after
Assisi. As Michael Adams notes: "There is no more cogent symbol than this of the continuity of Umbrian history."

In fact Monte Luco is the Mount Athos of Italy: a mountain
made sacred not by one or two but by three millenia of uninter-
rupted worship by ancient Umbrians and Romans, then by Syrian and Italian hermits and Benedictine monks and a diocesan
congregation of hermits, and for the last seven and a half centuries by contemplative sons of St. Francis who are still there
today in one of the finest of his twenty hermitages, now a thriving retreat center, like the Carceri. The rich monastic history of
Monte Luco will be briefly surveyed in *Forefathers of St. Francis*
(see also TJA 1–3).

The particular aspect of Monte Luco which interests us now in
connection with Umbria in Roman times is the dense forest of
oak and ilex trees on its summit which was a nature shrine of the
pagan religion of the Umbri. Mentioned with respect by Cato,
Seneca, and Pliny, it was accessible only after a rite of purifying
initiation. Pilgrims then suspended sacrificial incense vases and
other pottery as offerings on the branches of its venerated trees.
Still more significantly, with a special relevance for ecology, this
sacred forest was the subject of one of the oldest recorded laws
to protect the environment: the *Lex Spoletana,* a third-century
(B.C.) Roman decree engraved in archaic Latin on a large stone
column, still extant, which absolutely forbids, under severe
penalties, cutting down a single tree or even a branch.

The truly remarkable atmosphere of natural beauty and peace

which is still perceptible in this sacred forest has received the ultimate testimonial in its being chosen by St. Francis as the site of one of his favorite hermitages. But it has also earned other meaningful tributes.

Michelangelo found sorely needed peace of soul there. At the age of eighty-one the profoundly devout, even mystical genius wrote of his visit in 1556: "These days I have had great pleasure in the mountains of Spoleto in visiting those hermits, so that I have returned to Rome less than half myself, because truly we find peace only in the woods."

Even nowadays, according to the French art historian Marcel Brion, "the most worldly passerby cannot resist the religious emotion which grips him when he walks into that dense and dark forest" (Brion 82). I heartily agree.

III

Roman Assisi

The Augustan era, from 31 B.C. to A.D., 14, saw Roman civilization at the peak of its glory, with a galaxy of talented poets entertaining the unscrupulous but efficient emperor and his affluent courtiers: Virgil, Horace, Catullus—and Sextus Propertius, who was born in a prominent family in the prosperous *municipium* of Assisium about 50 B.C. His moody personality, troubled genius, and passionate elegies merit brief attention here not only because he spent his early and last years in Assisi, but still more for the striking contrasts between him and Assisi's most famous son and poet.

1 *Propertius, Assisi's First Great Poet*

Like St. Francis, Propertius was a true Umbrian in his lifelong affection for his homeland. Here is how he described his birthplace, addressing himself in the words of a soothsayer: "Ancient Umbria gave you birth in a noted household. . . . Do I hit upon the boundaries of your native land? Where foggy Mevania drips dew onto the hill-girdled plain, and the waters of the Umbrian lake turn warm in summer, and the wall of Assisi climbs steeply to the slope's summit, that wall rendered more famous by your genius" (*Carmina,* IV.1.121–126). The Roman Mevania is now

Bevagna, a few miles west of Foligno. (On the Umbrian lake, see iv.3.)

The childhood of Propertius in Assisi was traumatized by tragedy. He wrote: "Perugia gave my father a field of death and a tomb." In 40 B.C., when the boy was ten, Perugia was besieged for seven months by the future Augustus, then named Octavianus, because it had sided with his rival Mark Anthony (who was about to become involved with Cleopatra in Egypt). Famine finally forced the Perugians to yield, and as a penalty three hundred leading citizens were executed. That night, before the sacking scheduled for the next day, one of them set his house on fire, and a strong wind spread the flames until the entire city burned to the ground.

Later the poet grieved: "In Italy's hour of affliction, when civil strife drove Rome's citizens against one another—ah, hills of Etruria, you gave me sorrow beyond measure, for you let the limbs of my kinsman be cast aside unburied and denied a handful of soil to cover his bones" (*Carmina,* I.22.3ff). In that civil strife his family lost their estates in Umbria, and the widow and her son moved to Rome.

Propertius' first book of poems won him a place among the brilliant Augustan literati and entry into the sophisticated circle of the millionnaire Maecenas. The young poet became a lover of the famous Cynthia, a cultured upper-class courtesan. But after that affair soured and she died, he returned to Umbria, whose rural charm he evoked in verse, praising its white oxen and timorous hare and birds, joking that he carefully avoided the dangerous boars. He died in Assisi after 16 B.C. An ancient mausoleum, beyond the walls on the way down to San Damiano, is known locally as "the Tomb of Propertius."

The passionate personality of Propertius, as reflected in his elegies—couplets of hexameters followed by pentameters, more or less mournful in mood—offers a sharp contrast to that of Assisi's second famous poet, St. Francis. Yet perhaps the Poverello would comment: "There, but for the grace of God, go I. . . ."

Pale, thin, even sickly, Propertius remained foppish and sensual all his life. Over-emotional and sentimental, he made a career of love and love poetry. Fantasy and humor often redeemed his egotism and vanity. To Cynthia he wrote: "Caesar won glory in war, but what are all his conquered peoples compared to love? . . . No child of ours will ever become a soldier."

He was gifted with a sensuous feeling for beauty, combined with a moody, even morbid melancholy. His gloomy, pagan philosophy, steeped in a haunted sense of death's fatality, echoes in this key line: "A long night is coming for you, and never again will day return."

Perhaps significantly, his troubled verses have enjoyed a rebirth of popularity in modern times. The great German poet-philosopher Goethe (see next Section and Appendix A) liked to tap out the rhythms of Propertius' hexameters with his fingers. He was also a favorite of Ezra Pound, whose *Homage to Sextus Propertius* has been called "a supreme example of creative translation" that brings out the "modern" qualities of Assisi's first great poet.

2 *The Temple of Minerva, Described by Goethe*

Assisi has a good number of Roman remains: walls, an amphitheater, forum, tombs and sarcophagi, inscriptions and pieces of sculpture, with a notable Roman Museum. During its centuries as a *municipium*, it merited at least a passing mention in the writings of the elder Cato, Pliny the Younger, Strabo, and others.

Like all Roman towns, it had temples honoring various gods: a Temple of Janus on the lower slope where the Vescovado and first cathedral Santa Maria were built; a Temple of the *Bona Mater*, Good Mother, on the upper hill where the second cathedral of San Rufino is located; a Temple of Hercules still farther up; and a Temple of Mars below that of Janus.

But the finest and most important of all was the simple, handsome Temple of Minerva, Goddess of Wisdom, that was erected under Augustus (before A.D. 14) overlooking the center of the city from the upper side of the Piazza or main square.

Probably St. Francis himself admired its "Franciscan" beauty-in-simplicity and the symmetry of its portico adorned with six Corinthian columns. He may well have preached some of his popular sermons standing between those ancient columns, as so ably predicted by the great Chilean artist Pedro Subercaseaux Errazuriz in his album of fifty magnificent watercolor paintings, *Saint Francis of Assisi* (Chicago, 1976).

Let us now enjoy this description of the Temple by its most famous and fervent admirer, Johann Wolfgang von Goethe, written in Foligno on the evening of his memorable one-day visit to Assisi on October 26, 1786, which we will narrate fully in Appendix A from his *Letters from Italy:*

> Behold! Before my eyes stood the noble edifice—the first complete memorial of antiquity I had ever seen. A modest temple, as befitting so small a town, and yet so perfect, so well conceived, that it would be an ornament anywhere.
>
> First, as to its site. Since I had read in Vitruvius and Palladio how towns should be built, and how temples and public structures should be located, I have had great respect for such things. And how grand the ancients were in relation to Nature! The temple stands about halfway up the hill, where two hillocks meet, on a level place that is still called the Piazza. This even rises slightly, and four streets come together there, making an extended St. Andrew's cross, two coming from below, two from above. Probably in ancient times the houses that now stand opposite the temple, blocking the view, had not yet been built. If we remove them mentally, then one could see toward

the south over a most fertile countryside, and at the same time the Temple of Minerva would be visible from all sides. . . .

Gazing at the façade, I could not sufficiently admire the architects' genius for consistency here too. The order is Corinthian, with the distance between the columns about two modules. The bases of the columns and the plinths seem to rest on pedestals, but only apparently. The plinth is cut through in five places; and at each place, five steps ascend between the columns and bring one to the level where the columns actually rest and from which one enters the temple. The bold idea of cutting through the plinth was the right thing to do here; for as the temple is set on a hill, the steps leading up to it would have had to extend much too widely and would have made the square's area narrower. . . .

Unwillingly I tore myself away from the sight, and resolved to call the attention of all architects to this building, so that we may obtain an accurate draft of it. . . . Its aspect is so full of repose and beauty as to satisfy both the mind and the eye. What evolved within me from contemplating this work of art cannot be expressed and will bring forth imperishable fruits.

The subsequent history of this little Roman temple is of importance to all who are interested in Assisi. By the eleventh century it belonged to the Benedictine monks of San Benedetto Abbey on the slope south of the town, and they used it as their city house and office. In fact they had some *camerae et casae*, compartmented rooms, in the portico, between the columns (FNV III, 13, 579). During the career of St. Francis, on May 24, 1212, the monks signed a deed formally transferring the building to the city government for use as Assisi's new town hall by the *podestà*, consuls, and *priori* (successive titles of the mayors or city managers), who had hitherto used quarters near San

Rufino. Also at this time the city jail was installed in the cellar of the former temple. Official documents were henceforth signed and witnessed (in good weather) in the portico beyond the columns.

In about 1300, Giotto and his pupils painted the Minerva (with only five columns and a nonexistant small rose window) in the scene of the young man honoring Francis before his conversion by spreading his cloak before his feet, in the series of frescos on the walls of the Upper Church of San Francesco. They also anachronistically included the base of the adjoining tower, the Torre del Popolo, which was begun in 1274 and completed in 1305.

The Minerva served as city hall for a century, until in 1317 the citizens erected a larger Palazzo dei Priori on the opposite side of the Piazza. In 1339 the former temple was re-opened as a chapel of the Confraternity of Our Lady, then enlarged and made into the Church of Santa Maria sopra Minerva in 1539, later remodeled in Baroque style in 1634, and dedicated to St. Philip Neri in 1758.

The church has been served by priests of the Third Order Regular of St. Francis from 1613 to 1758 and since 1918. The Oratorian Fathers were in charge from 1758 to 1810, with secular priests during the nineteenth century. Its history has been compiled by Padre Pietro Chioccioni, T.O.R. (see Bibliography).

Postscript. We must add this little postscript to Roman Assisi, because it has a very indirect link to—of all people—Pietro di Bernardone, the father of St. Francis.

Just off the Piazza, in the crypt of the former church of San Nicolo where Francis, Bernard, and Peter Catani consulted the Gospels three times, is a rich Roman Museum. Among the exhibits, including tombstones, column capitals, urns, and statuary, is a lapidary inscription which commemorates the dedication of a small Temple of Castor and Pollux by proudly proclaiming the financial gifts of a rich citizen of Roman Assisi and his wife: "With their money they had the tetrastyle monument and the statues of Castor and Pollux made, and gave them as a gift to the Municipality of Assisi, and at the dedication they gave the City Officials fifteen silver coins each and to the people ten each."

The inscription is not dated, but the year could have been about the same when on a hill overlooking the lovely Sea of Galilee an unknown prophet from Nazareth inaugurated a spiritual revolution by declaring: "When you give alms, do not sound a trumpet before you, as the hypocrites do in the streets, so that they may be praised by men" (Mt 6:2).

St. Francis no doubt never saw this inscription, which in his time probably lay some feet underground. But he perceived the wealthy donors' new-rich psychology in the soul of his bourgeois father, Pietro di Bernardone . . . and in his own heart before he came to know Christ and His Gospel.

It was not many years after the dedication of that temple that the Gospel of the Galilean prophet came first to Rome from the Holy Land and then up the Via Flaminia into Umbria and Assisi, to bear especially abundant fruit in souls there.

INTERLUDE
SPRINGS OF LIVING WATERS

IV

The Clitunno River Springs and Temple
"A Franciscan Landscape"
from Roman River-god Cult
to Christian Baptism Shrine

1 Introduction

If you happen to be driving between Assisi and Spoleto, take special care not to rush right by one of the most beautiful sites in Italy—hence in Europe or the world—without even noticing it.

Just off the highway about five miles south of Foligno and north of Spoleto, on the right (west) going south, all that the hurried and uninformed tourist may glimpse is a small grove of poplar trees behind a stone wall with a gate and a sign reading FONTI DEL CLITUNNO. But you will be unaware that this grove marks one of the most famous spots in classical antiquity, praised in verse by Virgil and Propertius, Byron and Carducci, and painted by artists like Poussin and Corot.

It might truly be called a pagan poets' paradise-like park. And it has rightly been termed "a Franciscan landscape" by Father Agostino Gemelli, O.F.M.

We can be sure that St. Francis often hiked by this grove while traveling on foot between Assisi and Spoleto. While no incident recorded in his biographies is directly related to the place, we know that he spent a night being tormented by demons in the Benedictine Church of San Pietro di Bovara just off the highway two miles away, and that he imposed silence on a braying "Brother Donkey" in the square of the hilltown of Trevi another two miles north. We will see at the end of this Interlude that the deeper, mystical significance of this Roman and Christian sacred site forms an essential element in his spirituality and message, and also that it throws light on a crucial aspect of the Franciscan appreciation of beauty in nature.

By all means, therefore, we should heed these "stop-look-and-admire" warnings of four among a dozen major writers who have relished and described this lovely site. (Their works are listed in the Bibliography under UMBRIA—DESCRIPTION and CLITUNNO SPRINGS.)

"See it! Everything will delight you. I am only sorry I delayed so long seeing it." Pliny the Younger.

"It is a place too beautiful for any to pass by." Edward Hutton.

"Pass not unblest the Genius of the place!" Byron.

"It is not a place which one glances at in passing." Marcel Brion.

So we shall follow their advice and make a leisurely visit to these Springs and the nearby small Early Christian Temple, because in more than one way both epitomize and resume the religious history of Umbria in Roman and Early Christian times.

After quoting some descriptions of the principal features of the Springs and their surrounding park, we will survey their popularity and fame in classical antiquity. Also the relation of the Clitunno River to the (now-drained) Umbrian lake below Assisi and to the Tiber Riber. Then we will examine in some detail the little Temple, because it is one of the most important Early Christian churches in Italy. Lastly we must reflect on the spiritual significance of Springs and Temple in relation to the spirituality of St. Francis, particularly as outlined by Father Gemelli in reacting against a famous poem on the Springs by the great modern Italian writer Giosuè Carducci.

2 The Springs: A Pagan Poets' Paradise-like Park

The following general description of the site is as accurate
today as it was when written around the year A.D. 100 by the
Roman orator and consul Pliny the Younger in his *Letters* (VIII,
8). Incidentally he owned a large country estate in Umbria,
north of Città di Castello, overlooking the Upper Tiber River
valley:

> There is a fair-sized hill which is densely wooded
> with ancient cypresses; at the foot of this the spring
> rises and gushes out through several channels of dif-
> ferent size, and when its eddies have subsided, it
> broadens out into a pool as clear as glass. . . . Then it is
> carried on, not by any downward slope of the land but
> by its own volume and weight of water. . . . The banks
> are clothed with ash trees and poplars, whose green
> reflections can be counted in the clear stream as if
> they were planted there.

Now, before going into detail, here are some of the general
impressions reported by visitors: "A delicious site . . . exquisite . . . delightful . . . lovely . . . a warm and gentle scene . . . a
marvelously romantic spot . . . one of the most charming and
romantic spots in Umbria . . . a timelessly arcadian spot . . . a
pretty outcrop of classicism in a medieval land."

Next, several specific features: the spring and its waters, the
pond or lake with tiny islands, the trees, etc.

The Springs

"Out of the limestone mountain, spurting from under the leap
of the Flaminian Way, a score of springs form themselves
straightway into pools so silent and untroubled that you would
swear they have no movement at all; and yet the water, after
enfolding grassy islands, runs away into the fields, a full-grown

river at the very point of its birth" (Ernest Raymond). "The river springs straight from the foot of the hills—a limpid stream, rising almost invisibly through the grass and trees which overshadow its mysterious source" (Symonds). "The spring itself, bubbling up clearly and quietly . . . like a continuous emanation of magic from the earth" (Harrison). "In the calm pool I watch the slender spring as it rises: it sways, and a slight surge stirs the waters' mirror" (Carducci).

The Water

Several writers have noted its extraordinary transparency. "As clear as glass. You can count the coins which have been thrown in and the pebbles shining at the bottom" (Pliny). "We saw the Clitumnus, so recently from its source in the marble rock, that it was still as pure as a child's heart, and as transparent as truth itself" (Hawthorne). "But thou Clitumnus! in thy sweetest wave / Of the most living crystal that was e'er / . . . gentle waters! And most serene of aspect, and most clear" (Byron).

Also, Pliny reported that "the water is as cold and as sparkling as snow." And so Edward Hutton found it when bathing in it eighteen hundred years later.

The Lake

"An exquisite pool, very shallow, unruffled . . . an emerald-green lake which reflects the sky's blue tint . . . a curious glass-green light." Several small plank bridges connect its few grass-covered islets.

The Trees

Ash, alder, poplars, cypresses, and weeping willows. "Poplars guard the solitude everywhere, and willows bend like Melisande to weep over the dark water" (Raymond). "The vertical lines of the waving poplars give a boundless nobility to this scene which seems like a dream" (Secret). "Tall poplars, sensitive to the slightest impulses of the breeze, murmur in our ears their unending secrets and create an authentically religious atmosphere" (Brion). "A solemn, holy grove."

Carducci noted the colorful flowers amid the grass: "The flowers seem like sapphires and sparkle like inflexible diamonds and cooly shine and call to the silence of the green depths."

Only Byron mentions the fish in the "current's calmness; oft from out it leaps / The finny darter with the glittering scales, / Who dwells and revels in thy glassy deeps; / While, chance, some scatter'd water-lily sails / Down where the shallower wave still tells its bubbling tales."

Ada Harrison observed "scintillating sapphire-and-black dragonflies trying their first flight above the water."

A few snow-white serene swans appear in recent photographs of the little pond.

Virgil and other Roman writers referred to the "white flocks" of sheep and the large white oxen that were led to be washed in the stream, and some modern visitors have seen remote descendants of those cattle placidly grazing on the river banks.

In fact six classical Roman poets penned a total of seventeen lines about the Clitumnus Springs and their River-god of that name, with seven references to the oxen. Those poets are Virgil, Propertius, Statius, Silius Italicus, Juvenal, and Claudian. Only the first two display any warmth and color.

The background is always the traditional assembling of the great white oxen at nearby Bovara (from the Latin *boves*, oxen), followed by their ritual bathing in the springs' purifying waters, before being conducted to participate in triumphal processions in Rome.

As Virgil put it in his *Georgics* (III, 146):

Hence your snowy flocks, Clitumnus, and the bulls,

> Noblest victims, so often bathed in your sacred
>   stream,
> Have led Rome's triumphal processions to the tem-
>   ples of the gods.

Only the Umbrian Propertius, son of Assisi (see III.1), evokes,
yet with only one warm word, the beauty of the site (*Elegies,* II,
xix, 25):

> Where Clitunus shrouds his fair streams in his grove
> And laves with his waters the snow-white kine.

It is interesting that Pliny fails to mention the oxen in his
lengthy description of the Springs, perhaps because none were
present during his visit. However, he supplies additional information which indicates that the shrine of the river-god was then
a popular resort and center of pilgrimages:

> Closely by is a holy temple of great antiquity in
> which is standing an image of the god Clitumnus him-
> self clad in a magistrate's bordered robe. The written
> oracles lying there prove the presence and prophetic
> powers of his divinity. All around are a number of
> small shrines, each containing its god and having its
> own name and cult, and some of them also their own
> springs, for as well as the parent stream there are
> smaller ones which afterward join the river. The
> bridge that spans it marks the sacred water off
> from the ordinary stream: above the bridge only boats
> are allowed, while below bathing is also permitted.
> The people of Hispellum (Spello), to whom the
> deified Emperor Augustus presented the site, main-
> tain a bathing place at the town's expense and also
> provide an inn; and there are several houses pic-
> turesquely situated along the river bank. . . . You can
> study the numerous inscriptions in honor of the

spring and the god which many hands have written
on every pillar and wall . . . some will make you laugh.

3 The River: the Clitunno Flows into "Father Tiber"

Pliny also indicates that the Clitunno River was broader in
Roman times, before an earthquake reduced its flow in the fifth
century A.D.:

> One minute it is still a spring and the next a broad
> river navigable for boats to which it can give passage
> even when two are moving in opposite directions and
> must pass each other. The current is so strong that
> although the ground remains level, a boat travelling
> downstream is hurried along without needing its oars,
> while it is very difficult to make any headway up-
> stream with oars and poles combined. Anyone boat-
> ing for pleasure can enjoy hard work alternating with
> easy movement simply as a change of course.

Now if we follow the course of the Clitunno northward along
the Valley of Spoleto, we find that, with two parallel streams, it
runs past Bevagna and joins the Topino at Cannara, where St.
Francis preached to the birds (LF Chap. 16). A few miles beyond
Cannara the Chiascio River runs into the Topino, and they both
flow into the Tiber at Torgiano south of Perugia. And Dante
tells us that the Chiascio's "waters descend from the hill chosen
by Blessed Ubaldo," Patron Saint of Gubbio, whom we will meet
in *Forefathers of St. Francis* (*Paradiso* 11.44; cf TJA 218).

This confluence of several rivers brings us to what Propertius
and other classical writers called the *lacus Umber,* the Umbrian
lake, now emptied, which flooded much of the plain between
Perugia and Assisi and Bettona in Roman times, until its waters

were drained by engineers under the Ostrogoth Arian King Theodoric (who died in 526, a year after executing the philosopher Boethius). Writing perhaps in Assisi, Propertius evoked in one vivid line "the summer heat warming the waters of the Umbrian lake" (*Elegies,* IV, I, 124).

According to several ancient historians, in prehistoric times vast areas of the Central Umbrian valleys were flooded, to the point where the name of the earliest inhabitants, the *Umbri,* was said to be derived from the Greek word *ombroi,* meaning "bathed" or "saved from the waters or rains." So the Lombard historian Paul the Deacon (fl. 790) wrote in his *History of the Lombards* (II, 16): "In Umbria are found Perugia and the Lake of Clitorius (Clitumnus) and Spoleto. For it is called Umbria because it survived the flooding when once a watery disaster devasted the inhabitants."

Geological studies have in fact established that during the Pliocene epoch at the end of the glacial era the Tiber formed an immense lake on the central plain of Umbria. Gradual erosion forced a passage through the deep gorge in the hills below Todi known as the Forello.

However, the Umbrian lake of Roman times was made not by the Tiber but by the flowing together of the Clitunno, Topino, and Chiascio rivers around the town of Bastia, which was then called Isola (Island) Romana. Even today the Topino may overflow its banks during the winter rains, and much of the soil between Bevagna and Bettona consists of swamps and bogs, crisscrossed by dikes and moats (see Richmond 169).

Incidentally, speaking of Bastia, it was to the Benedictine Convent of San Paolo di Bastia that St. Francis took St. Clare after her vesting as the first Poor Lady at the Portiuncola. That convent was located north of Bastia, where the Tescio torrent flows from behind Assisi (below its lonely cemetery) into the Chiascio. Later in the thirteenth century the nuns moved within the walls of the city for security, as did the Poor Clares of San

Damiano. Another Franciscan link with Bastia is that one of the "bright stars and heavenly men" of the *Fioretti,* Blessed Conrad of Offida, died there in 1306 (see LF Chaps. 42 and 43).

A comically fantastic footnote to the prehistoric flooding of Umbria was supplied by an imaginative local chronicler in the seventeenth century, a time when prosperous cities and families paid high prices for fancy and fanciful local histories and genealogies tracing their "roots" back to famous heroes of antiquity or of the Bible. So the Perugian Franciscan Fra Felice Ciatti boldly transformed Paul the Deacon's "watery disaster" into "the Universal Deluge" of Genesis and claimed that Noah himself came with his sons to Italy after the Flood and founded Perugia (Heywood 6).

Still following the downward flow of the clear, cold waters of the Clitunno with those of the Topino and Chiascio to their junction with the Tiber, we should not conclude this chapter without a few lines of tribute to that masterful "Father Tiber" which forms a liquid spine of Umbria and Franciscan Italy. Along or near its banks, from Pieve San Stefano below La Verna past Perugia down to Orte, lie the sites of too many incidents in the life of St. Francis to list here.

But for all who love Umbria because it was his beloved homeland on this earth, I strongly recommend a book which vividly describes the course of the Tiber River through much of that province from a unique viewpoint. This is *Down the Tiber and Up to Rome* by Eberlein, Marks, and Wallis (see Bibliography). Those three young men are perhaps the only persons ever to float down the river on an inflated rubber-boat from Perugia to Rome and to describe the exciting journey in a colorful, literate, and entrancing narrative, including chapters on the Upper Tiber valley above Perugia. A noteworthy element in their account is their frequent contacts with local inhabitants, especially villagers, whom they report to be simple, kindly, friendly, cheerful, hospitable, and amiable—in other words, Franciscan. This is certainly one of the best books ever written on Umbria.

Since the Tiber flows through Umbria and so is connected with St. Francis, I will quote from that fine book this striking "profile" of "Father Tiber":

> Father Tiber is a very temperamental river. One day he can be tame and harmless. The next, he can be a raging torrent. He can be an agreeable enough companion, so long as you accept him as he is and fall in willingly with his changing moods. He is imperious, wayward and willful. To know Father Tiber in his true character, you must follow his course from his rugged birthplace in the heart of the high Appennines, past Perugia and through the Umbrian plain, through ii Forello and the mountain fastnesses between that savage gorge and Orte. . . . If you have not yet yielded to the glamour of those mystic and little-known parts of Italy through which much of his seaward journey lies, and if you have not yet conceived a genuine affection for him, you will at least have learned to hold him in profound respect. *Father* Tiber you can fitly call him; you instinctively feel that he is far too august and reverend ever to be familiarly alluded to as 'Old Man River.'

St. Francis, we know, had a special chaste affection for Sister Water. And he actually chose a scenic spot along the banks of Father Tiber for one of his twenty hermitages: that of Pantanelli, south of Orvieto, between the lower end of the new artificial Lake of Corbara and the great Florence-to-Rome Autostrada del Sole. There the enduring local tradition points out a Grotto, Spring, Garden, and ilex Tree—all "of St. Francis." And there the Poverello is said to have climbed onto a massive rock beside the flowing Tiber to preach a sermon to the fishes. This shady *ritiro* of Pantanelli is also closely associated with the famous Franciscan poet Jacopone da Todi. It is still a friary today. Its history has been thoroughly documented by Father Livarius Oliger, O.F.M.

4 The Tiny Temple
One of Umbria's First Christian Churches

As if the unique charm and beauty of the Clitunno's sparkling springs and park were not enough, just one kilometer north, on the western edge of the highway, and also easily not noticed, stands a small building which has been called "the most interesting monument of late antiquity in Umbria . . . the most gracious Early Christian church in Umbria . . . a jewel of Early Christian art . . . unique of its kind."

Or as Lord Byron aptly put it in his stanzas on the springs and their river-god in *Childe Harold's Pilgrimage:*

> And on thy happy shore a Temple still,
> Of small and delicate proportion, keeps
> Upon a mild declivity of hill,
> Its memory of thee . . .

Over half a dozen observant writers have been entranced by the almost "Franciscan" simplicity and beauty of this "tiny, elegant, graceful, delightful, informal provincial temple . . . a beautifully proportioned building, in a wonderful state of preservation . . . everything about it is unusual . . . its architecture is sober and rustic. . . . Standing alone above the clear river that flows away from the springs. . . . Here was the actual shrine of the god . . . and here it was rebuilt into the tiny columned temple that still stands, like a summer-house in stone, on the high bank."

Pliny mentioned "a holy temple of great antiquity" and a

number of small shrines. However, experts do not believe that the present Temple was one of those, but rather was built, probably using some of their stones and columns, originally perhaps as a late classical temple around the year A.D. 400, then eventually completed in its upper structure as an Early Christian church in the fifth or seventh century, with some restoration work as late as the twelfth century.

Thus the little Temple of the Clitunno is one of the first of Umbria's five surviving Early Christian churches. It was evidently erected at the same time as Spoleto's San Salvatore and (original) San Pietro, and perhaps before the two circular churches: Terni's San Salvatore and Perugia's remarkable Sant'Angelo, both of the fifth century.

The Tempietto del Clitunno was also called in the past San Salvatore or San Crocifisso. The title of the central church was San Salvatore, while the two smaller side-chapels were dedicated respectively to St. John the Baptist and St. Michael the Archangel.

Significant of the spirituality of Umbria's early Christians are the striking inscriptions on the three friezes (two now lost, but copied in extant notes):

SANCTUS DEUS ANGELORUM QUI FECIT RESURREC-
TIONEM
SANCTUS DEUS PROPHETARUM QUI FECIT SAL-
VATIONEM
SANCTUS DEUS APOSTOLORUM QUI FECIT REDEMP-
TIONEM

(Holy God of the Angels who accomplished the Resurrection. Holy God of the Prophets who accomplished the Salvation. Holy God of the Apostles who accomplished the Redemption.)

Equally significant is the symbolism used in the skilled decorative sculpting of the three pediments, which includes monogrammed crosses adorned with leaves amid vine tendrils and clusters of grapes.

Goethe stopped by while passing the Temple on the day after his memorable visit to Assisi in 1786 (see III.2 and Appendix A), and he penned in his *Letters from Italy* one of the most acute comments of the many which we have on the architecture of the Temple: "San Crocifisso, a strange chapel by the roadside, I do not consider the remains of a temple that stood on the site, rather they found columns, pillars, pediments, and flung them together not stupidly but insanely. It simply cannot be described, though somewhere there is an engraving of it."

Confirming his judgment, modern scholars have noted several surprising, i.e., nonclassical features. The materials used include a variety of marble, limestone, and travertine blocks. Only one of the two convoluted columns is monolithic. The capitals do not match. And the two pairs of outer pillars are not found in temples of this type in the classical period.

These irregularities explain why Goethe as a strict neoclassicist admired the pure design of Assisi's Augustan era Temple of Minerva, while disdaining the Tempietto of the Clitunno (see III.2). Incidentally both have six columns.

In the interior the design of the *cella* reveals Oriental, specifically Syrian, features in the pediment with finely sculptured cornices and in the four small windows. Similar Oriental elements also appear in the contemporary San Salvatore Basilica near Spoleto, proving the presence there in the fifth century of monks and craftsmen from Syria. The most outstanding and best documented instance of this Syrian presence in Umbria is the monk St. Isaac of Spoleto (d. 525), who was known to informants of St. Gregory the Great and who founded the first Christian hermitage on Monte Luco (see II.4, TJA Index, and *Forefathers*).

The small apse—part of the original structure and another

nonclassical feature—contains above the plain altar a remarkable set of paintings dating back to the seventh or eighth century. Restored in 1932 yet fading, they are considered the oldest
Christian paintings in Umbria, and as such merit close attention.

First, in the semicircular ceiling of the apse, appears a large
cross with gem in the center and on each side busts of angels.
Beneath the pediment, in a smaller apse, is a handsome bearded
Christ of the Pantocrator (Almighty Sovereign) type of Byzantine churches, holding in His left hand the open Book of the
Gospel. Below him, on either side of a tiny niche with triangular
top, are fresco paintings of Saints Peter (left) and Paul (right),
the former with white hair and beard, the latter dark.

Here in these several examples of the earliest Christian art in
Umbria we may note a number of features that later re-appear
in the spirituality of St. Francis: the Redeemer Jesus Christ with
his saving Gospel and Cross, his Angels and Chief Apostle Peter.
Also the leaves and grapes as gifts of Mother Earth.

But probably the most meaningful element of all in the Temple, both in itself and in relation to St. Francis, is to be found in
the reality and symbol of the pure, cleansing waters of the
springs and river, which the early Christians of the region put to
fruitful spiritual use as sacramental channels of God's grace.

For according to an important local oral tradition, recorded in
1643 by the convert German traveler and antiquarian Lukas
Holste (Holstenius), "the inhabitants report that the early Christians of Umbria were washed in baptism here." Thus as L.
Fausti, a modern Spoleto historian, wrote, "If we think of the
early custom of baptizing alongside rivers, as did the Baptist,
and of the care which the Church had to implant the cult of the
True Faith where that of false idols had prevailed, we will find
the explanation of churches of San Salvatore and the Baptistery
of John bathed by the waters of the sacred river of Umbria."
Another historian, A. Sansi, noted that "the waters of the

Clitunno, famed for the white color which they gave to oxen, came to be used in baptism to make souls white." As Monsignor Fabbi neatly sums it up: "The sacred water [of the Clitunno] became the Jordan River of Christian Umbria" (Fabbi 120, 220).

In this connection we know that the Springs and the pagan Temple were a popular regional shrine not only by Pliny's testimony but also by the fact that in the year A.D. 333 the site was identified in itineraries of the Via Flaminia (see II.3) as *ad sacraria* (the shrines or chapels).

A few years later the Roman Emperor Constantine issued an important rescript authorizing the city of Spello to erect a temple to serve for the annual Umbrian festivals and games, so that the people of the region would not have to travel over the mountains to the traditional Etruscan shrine at Vulsinii near Orvieto. Historians do not agree on whether this new temple was the Tempietto of the Clitunno. The site belonged to Spello, though closer to Spoleto. The little Temple would seem to be too small for such regional celebrations. Yet the site itself, on a hillside overlooking the plain and near the highway, was appropriate. In any case, soon afterward, probably not long after the year 400, the present Temple was built as one of Umbria's first and most memorable Christian churches.

And there it has stolidly stood on its hillside looking over St. Francis' beloved because lovely Valley of Spoleto for the past sixteen centuries, witnessing the rise and decline of empires and duchies and counties, and the coming and going of popes and bishops and abbots and saints and sinners. . . .

In the year 1155 the famous German Emperor Frederick Barbarossa (red beard) camped with his army by the Clitunno river and springs when he attacked and sacked Spoleto because it took hostage his envoy and assaulted his troops. But to his ruthless destruction and burning of the city, Spoleto owes the subsequent building of its beautiful "new" cathedral, whose handsome façade, like that of San Rufino in Assisi (see XXI), was being completed during the lifetime of St. Francis. And the Duomo of Spoleto guards among its treasures (besides Francis' moving Letter to Brother Leo; see Omn 118) a venerated Byzantine icon of the Madonna without Child which Barbarossa gave the city in 1185 as a token of reconciliation (Fabbi 142–44).

When Napoleon Bonaparte conquered Central Italy in 1798, he organized a regional "Department of the Clitunno" in Umbria.

On taking leave of this very admirable, even lovable Tempietto of the Clitunno, I cannot resist adapting and applying to it these enthusiastic lines which Goethe wrote in 1786 about its twin, Assisi's Temple of Minerva: "The beautiful Temple once more caught my eye to soothe and console me. . . . Unwillingly I tore myself from the sight . . . the noble edifice . . . a modest temple, yet so well conceived that it would be an ornament anywhere. . . . Its aspect is so full of repose and beauty as to satisfy both the mind and the eye."

And the soul, we add. For more deeply than Assisi's Temple of pagan Wisdom, this little Early Christian church delights the friends of St. Francis because, with its limpid Springs, it embodies and conveys much of his humble spirituality, as the next three Sections of this Chapter will explain.

5 The Spirit of the Place:
A Shrine of Nature-Mystics

According to ancient Roman religious belief, the springs, temples, and park of the Clitumnus were actually indwelt by the spirit of the River-god of that name. It is also noteworthy that in Imperial Roman times the reputation of that god for auguries or fortune-telling attracted visits by two Emperors, Caligula (d. A.D. 41) and Honorius (d. 423).

At its best the old Roman religion cultivated a spirit of awe, devotion, and gratitude toward the gods for their gifts to humans of fire, water, and the produce of Mother Earth. (Does this spirit re-echo in the Canticle of Brother Sun?) And that cult of the sacredness of nature was often concentrated in specific places which became shrines. We have two striking examples of such holy sites close to Spoleto (within twenty miles of Assisi): the Sacred Forest on Monte Luco (see II.5), and the Springs of the Clitunno.

But what are we to think of the surprising claims of half a dozen cultured modern writers that they have sensed at the Springs a truly religious atmosphere or spirit or "vibrations," as Michelangelo and Marcel Brion did on Monte Luco? As the Romans would say, *numen inest:* a divine presence indwells the place. Let us quote some of these testimonials before evaluating their significance.

First, the world-weary, haughty yet charming young English poet Lord Byron (d. 1824) gave three stanzas of Canto IV of his long poem, *Childe Harold's Pilgrimage,* to the Springs, Temple, and spirit of the Clitumnus. In the last of the three he paid this tribute of thanks to the god and to nature for their ability to suspend there his inner malaise:

> Pass not unblest the Genius of the place!
> If through the air a zephyr more serene
> Win to the brow, 't is his; and if ye trace
> Along his margin a more eloquent green,
> If on the heart the freshness of the scene
> Sprinkle its coolness, and from the dry dust
> Of weary life a moment lave it clean
> With Nature's baptism,—'t is to him ye must
> Pay orisons for this suspension of disgust.

Let us note in passing the relevant reference to "Nature's baptism" by this gifted poet who claimed that he was a believer . . . in his own free-spirited concept of Christianity. Yet he failed to mention St. Francis or Assisi in the hundred lines on Umbria in his poem.

For two other British lovers of Italy, Margaret Symonds and Lina Duff Gordon, "this marvelously romantic spot . . . seems to hold the very essence of what is best in pagan art and worship . . . one of the sweetest tributes that man's mind ever paid to the spirits of Nature."

Ada Harrison also reported that she sensed a certain spirit whose power grew on her during her visit. "A vestige of the god still lingers near the river . . . the spirit of poetry . . . and the place itself that caused that spirit to stir . . . must be one of the quietest spots on earth. Strangly enough . . . a spirit *is* abroad and grows gradually more potent, especially if one stays there through a hot and drowsy midday. . . . There is a certain tranquil charm for the eyes and a feeling of complete solitariness and abstraction from the world that is in itself a pleasure."

A Swiss-German traveler, Willy Meyer, was also struck by this timeless, other-worldly spirit of the place. "One does not anticipate what beauty is spread forth behind the trees. It grips us all of a sudden. By this spring and lake one day is like a thousand years. We no longer count the hours. The world beyond has slipped away from us like a useless, burdensome garment. We breathe. We gaze. We listen. We *are* . . ."

The perceptive French art critic Marcel Brion has given us an eloquent evocation of the site's enduring religious atmosphere in these lines:

It is impossible not to experience a moving sense of the sacred when one finds oneself in this spot charged with the devotion of the past. Even more than the

provincial and unpretentious temple, the streams that
flow among the reeds and meadows and the tall poplars, responding to the slightest impulses of the
breeze, murmur in our ears their timeless secrets and
create an authentically religious atmosphere with
which we associate ourselves by recollecting our
minds and hearts with the forces of nature. . . . I know
of no sight more friendly and kindly than that of the
Springs of the Clitunno, but this friendly aspect of
things, this kindliness of trees and water have in
themselves something divine that those who come
here cannot fail to feel (Brion 71–72).

This explicit perception of divinity in nature by both Christian
and unbelieving observers raises the interesting problem, very
relevant regarding St. Francis, of so-called nature-mysticism. It
has been ably studied by, among others, R. C. Zaehner in his
Mysticism, Sacred and Profane, and by Father David Knowles in
The Nature of Mysticism. The late Edward A. Armstrong left a
very rich study of *St. Francis: Nature Mystic,* which I warmly
welcomed in a review that we reprint in this book as Appendix B
to serve as an extension of this Chapter and to bring Armstrong's
work to your attention.

Here we must make a distinction between natural mysticism
and nature-mysticism. The first includes a wide variety of non-
supernatural, mind or soul expanding experiences, while the
second refers to experiences related to the beauty or power of
nature in creation. A significant aspect of both, for the Christian,
lies in their absence of a personal God.

In sharp contrast, the prophets and seers of the Old Testament and the New and the saints of the Church always perceived,
related to, and communed in nature with the God who created
it for mankind. And perhaps most profoundly of them all, St.
Francis of Assisi sought and found in nature's beauty and power

the reflection and the gift of God the Creator and Redeemer of
the human race—and of all groaning creation (see Appendix B:
Was St. Francis a "Nature Mystic"?).

6 *"A Franciscan Landscape"*
As Seen by Two Great Writers

The sharply contrasting reactions of two major Italian writers,
the poet Giosuè Carducci and Franciscan Father Agostino
Gemelli, to the spell and beauty of the Springs of the Clitunno
clearly illustrate the basic differences between the nonpersonal,
non-Christian appreciation of nature and the Christian, especially the Franciscan.

(A) Carducci

Giosuè Carducci (1835–1907), professor of Italian literature at
the University of Bologna for over forty years, was one of the
most gifted and influential of modern Italian poets. He was
awarded the Nobel Prize for Literature in 1906. His prose and
poetry forcefully opposed both decadent romanticism and religious asceticism, while extolling the virile ideals of the ancient
Romans. His volcanic and polemical temperament was reflected
in much of his writing.

But even his intense anticlericalism could not wholly resist the
charm of Umbria and St. Francis. Before going to Assisi, he had
hailed the Poverello in a speech as "a true Christian socialist."

In 1877 he wrote to a friend from Perugia: "The country here
is truly beautiful and such as the Umbrian school [of painters]
intimates: what lines on the horizon, what gradual evanescing of
vaporous mountains in the distance. I have been to Assisi: it is
something great, beautiful, a town, city, and shrine for one who

understands nature and art in their accord with history, with imagination, with human feeling. I am tempted to do two or three poems on Assisi and St. Francis."

In fact Carducci wrote three of his best poems on Umbrian subjects, though only one deals with St. Francis.

After visiting the Springs of the Clitunno in 1876, he wrote: "I will throw flowers into the sacred stream, but neither the god nor the nymph will respond to my evocations, nor show themselves to me... Yet these places are so beautiful and so filled with ancient Italy. Here one grasps something of even pre-Roman Italy."

Entranced by that beauty, he penned the first of his Umbrian poems, *Alle fonti del Clitunno.* It soon became a schoolbook classic which spotlighted the Springs near Spoleto as one of the most celebrated sites in Italy. Its 156 verses retrace the history of Umbria from the Etruscans through the Romans to the coming of Christianity. Hailed as one of the most majestic, lofty, and classical odes of nineteenth-century Italian literature, it evokes the cavalcade of historical eras by means of impressionistic sketches of landscapes. Above all it dramatizes—or rather caricatures—the contrast between the simple, hard-working, happy pagan peasants of antiquity and the "weird company" of early Christians, "singing litanies, robed in dark sackcloth.... Of the fields resounding with human labor ... they made a desert, and they called the desert the Kingdom of God.... Wherever the heavenly sun yielded blessings, they laid curses on the works of life and love...." The poem's last lines welcome the resurgence of modern Italy and "the steam of new industries."

A sojourn in Perugia a year later produced a more mellow "Song of Love" for the beauty of the Umbrian countryside. In this *Il canto dell'Amore,* the poet hears from the fields and hamlets, from churches that pray raising long marble arms to the sky, from houses and convents, streets and squares

Arise one single chant in a thousand songs,
One hymn, voicing a thousand prayers:
"Greeting O toiling humankind!
All things pass away and nothing can die.
Too much we hate and suffer. Love.
The world is beautiful and sacred is the future.

The peacemaking spirit of Umbria and Assisi's Saint even moved the anticlerical poet to this semihumorous gesture of reconciliation with his arch-foe Pope Pius IX (Giovanni Mastai-Ferretti): "Ten years ago I cursed the Pope. Now I would be reconciled with the Pope.... Come, Citizen Mastai, let's have a drink!"

Yielding further to the loving spirit of the Poverello, Carducci wrote to a friend: "Returning from the shrine of Assisi ... I would like to knock on the gate of the Convento at Assisi, and to the little friar asking what I want, answer, like Dante! 'Peace.'... O holy Father St. Francis, if you who were so good that you converted even the wolf ... if you were alive and interceded for me, who knows if even I would not be converted.... O Seraphic Father, if you were alive, I would confess to you ... and then we would sing some Praises together."

Nine years later Carducci wrote this fourteen-line tribute to St. Francis which has been called by one critic "the most beautiful poem in Italian literature":

Santa Maria degli Angeli
Brother Francis, how much air
This beautiful dome of Vignola embraces,
Where, arms crossed in your agony,
You lay naked on the ground only!

And July's heat throbs and the love song hovers
Above the labored plain. O that a trace
The song of Umbria might give me of your words,
The sky of Umbria give me of your face!

On the horizon of the hilltown,
In the mild, lonesome, lofty splendor,
Like the gates of your Paradise aloft,

I see you standing with arms outstretched
Singing to God: Praise to You, Lord,
For our sister bodily death!

Of this brief masterpiece another critic wrote: "Certainly no poet since Dante has caught in a few verses the soul of Francis bathed in the light of the Umbrian landscape and evoked in the two most human and Christian notes of his life: Lady Poverty and Sister Death." And Father Gemelli commented in his *Francescanesimo:* "Perhaps too in this greeting [the poet] caught a luminous glimpse of a Paradise that he knew not how to make his own. In this admirable sonnet Carducci, who is ever most intuitive when he reasons least, seems to wish to measure his own inferiority and that of his times in comparison to the great eras of faith."

In 1905, two years before he died, Carducci wrote in a kind of religious testament: "Every time I declaimed against Christ, it was out of hatred for priests. I do not admit the divinity of Christ. But certainly some expressions are too much. And without worshiping the divinity of Christ, I bow before the great human martyr."

That was as far as St. Francis was able to lead his brother poet.

(B) Gemelli

One of the great Catholic leaders of this century, Franciscan Father Agostino Gemelli (1878–1959) was born in Milan two years after Carducci wrote his poem on the Springs of the Clitunno. He was also in his youth an anticlerical socialist, but after becoming a doctor of medicine was converted and in 1908 ordained a priest. While teaching experimental psychology, he founded the Catholic University of the Sacred Heart in Milan in 1921 and remained its president until he died. More than any other institution, that University has renewed the faith of generations of young Italian men and women by placing knowledge in the service of love (see Maria Sticco's splendid biography in Bibliography).

Of direct relevance for this chapter and book, in 1937 Father Gemelli contributed an autobiographical article to *Vita e Pensiero* (*Life and Thought*, a monthly magazine of high intellectual quality which he founded and edited) in which he sharply criticized Carducci's famous poem on the Clitunno and described the place as a "Franciscan landscape." That four-page article attracted my attention to the Springs by the light it throws on the nature-mysticism of St. Francis in contrast to that of classical antiquity and its reflection in modern writers like Carducci.

Young Gemelli of course had studied the latter's poem in high school and even knew many of its melodious verses by heart forty years later. So on his first trip from Milan to Rome in the fall of 1890, he was delighted when his companion suggested that they visit the Springs of the Clitunno on the way.

But on seeing the little Temple and then the Springs, Gemelli was surprised to feel thoroughly disappointed, even disillusioned. The Temple seemed bare and insignificant, the Springs and stream also: *pocca cosa, povera cosa.* He recited aloud some of the poem's verses, "but the words fell within me void and without echo." Even the beauty of the natural setting failed to charm him: "I had not yet learned from St. Francis how to read in the great book of nature."

> "Shall we go to Assisi?" asked his companion.
> "What is of interest to see there?" he inquired.
> "It is the home of Francis of Assisi."
> "I'm not interested," said the future Franciscan.

At that time he knew only what he had read about the Saint in medieval history textbooks and Dante's *Divine Comedy.*

"Many, many years later," he wrote that he returned to the Clitunno, "how changed within and also without. Without, there is my habit which at every step reminds me of my sweet and beloved Franciscan vocation." And within he was cured of textbook classicism and the artificial outlook of intellectuals wrapped in a literary view of the world.

Above all I returned to the Springs of the Clitunno with that soul which St. Francis has made capable of understanding and reading in nature its deeper meaning. How the silent poplars and willow-trees of the Clitunno speak! How these crystalline and brown waters speak! How those surrounding hillsides speak, with their austere vegetation yet soft lines colored by the reflecting rays of the setting sun.

Nature becomes transformed in the Franciscan eye. Then in one's mind spontaneously arise the Praises of St. Francis singing of Brother Wind and Brother Sun and praising Sister Water. Later, as our eyes contemplate the various aspects of the landscape and seek to retain it for tomorrow (when in the bustling city our soul feels a need to recall pleasant memories and warm images), a gentle stir of emotion penetrates our inner depths. Now St. Francis teaches me to read in this charm of nature the reflection of a Divine Goodness which is the cause of all things. One thought leads to another, and before our eyes the ultimate meaning of life unfolds: the realization of a beauty that is never attained and can never be attained; such is the torment and the consolation of the soul which the vocation of Christian faith has made so exquisitely sensitive.

And the emotion which rises in our heart has its source in the thought that we too, as creatures of God, uplifted by God with grace, we too have an effective will for the good and the beauti-

ful. This is a great gift that God has given us: to be able to aspire
to beautiful and good and holy things, and to be able through
those aspirations to give life a lofty meaning.

Then, along that path, our soul glimpses between the poplars
and willows the shadow of Sister Death, which reminds us that
life is a passage, a struggle, a testing. But this thought does not
terrify us: for God helps us to understand that suffering and
death itself are seeds of life, since Sister Death introduces us
through pain to the true life.

This is the secret of nature in this Umbria. This is the language which it speaks to us when as pilgrims of love we visit this
Valley of Spoleto and there retrace the footsteps of our Father.

As a youth, deluded by the romantic fantasies of textbook
classicism, I was not aware that a few miles from the Springs of
the Clitunno had lived the man who taught how to read in nature her secret language of pain and death, of glory and holi-
ness, and of understanding the meaning of life. I had to come
back to those Springs with my Franciscan habit and without the
Carducci of my youth in order to appreciate the beauty of that
nature.

To this profound and wondrous insight into the living mystery of the Springs of the Clitunno, I can only add: Thank you
dear Father Francis, for having taught this great lesson to Father
Gemelli and through him to us!

7 *St. Francis and Living Waters*

We should conclude this Interlude on the Springs and Early
Christian Temple of the Clitunno with a few reflections on their
now evident relation to St. Francis and his spirituality.

The only reference to the Clitunno which I have found in his
modern biographies is the following in Father Murray Bodo's

beautiful and imaginative *Francis, The Journey and the Dream* (p. 7), dealing with his return to Assisi from Spoleto after the decisive "Master-or-servant" vision at the beginning of his conversion:

> He was returning to Assisi on the Roman Flaminian Way. The Roman legions had marched this same way, bold and confident in the power of Rome. They stopped and drank from the sacred Spring of Clitunno. They asked the water nymphs there to strengthen them in battle, to give them courage and victory.
>
> As Francis passed that same clear pool of water, the dream of glory drained from his heart, and war and victory were empty words rattling in his brain. He felt empty. Something told him that he was leaving the Roman way forever.... This was the most terrible experience of his early life.

Of course the familiar verse in the Canticle of Brother Sun praising Sister Water as "very useful and humble and precious and chaste" could have been inspired by the clear and limpid flow of the stream of the Clitunno ... or by the several springs which are said to have sprung from the ground at the Poverello's prayers.

In the Biblical Praises which he inscribed in the chapel of his Eremita Hermitage above Carsulae and Cesi, he included this line from Daniel (3:78): "Praise the Lord, all you rivers!"

We can be sure that St. Francis, in his strongly scriptural nature-mysticism, looked upon water with gratitude as a creature-gift of God to mankind. No doubt water meant to him much of what it stands for in the Bible.

As outlined in the rich article in the *Dictionnaire de Spiritualité* (DS 4.8–29), water as a source of life and fertility manifests God's goodness, and His power as an instrument of judgment in del-

uges, torrents, and floods. But most of all in the spirituality of
the New Testament it is a symbol of the Holy Spirit and of God's
grace, whether flowing in a stream from the Temple or from the
inner depths of the soul as the living waters of spiritual life given
freely. Also as a sacred sign in baptism and holy water, which the
Ritual for the latter calls "this sacred and innocent creature."

Father Eloi Leclerc's study of *The Canticle of Creatures*
(Chicago, 1977) includes a dense Chapter Seven on Sister Water
that abounds in psychological insights, some of which strike me
as too subtly Jungian to be simply Franciscan. Incidentally a very
rich collection of first-rate articles on the Canticle appeared in
the model Spanish Franciscan reader's digest *selecciones de Fran-
ciscanismo* (Apartado 7004, Valencia 3) enero-agosto 1976, Vol.
5, Nums. 13–14; I cannot recommend too strongly this splendid
review.

As for the park-like beauty of the Clitunno Springs, perhaps
when passing by the Little Poor Man of Assisi gratefuly praised
and thanked God for creating it and for the Eden-like garden of
his beloved Valley of Spoleto and for the whole world, His entire
beauty-drenched Creation which, as Francis said, God made for
man's sake (CA 51. SP 118), and where, as St. Bonaventure
added, "Every creature is a word of God, because it proclaims
God" (*Comm. in Eccl.;* vi, 16).

For that is an essential part of what Father Gemelli called and
magnificently formulated as the message of St. Francis to the
modern world, to our blindly self-centered and godlessly man-
centered contemporaries.

Two gifted French writers on Umbria provide profound insights into that message as related to the spirit and "Franciscan
landscape" of the Springs and the Valley of Spoleto.

First, the art critic Marcel Brion, in his excellent *L'Ombrie* (p.
82), referring to a spring of St. Francis on Monte Luco: "So it is
that over the summit of the sacred mountain of paganism blew

from Assisi the great Spirit of Love and Charity which was to transform the souls of men."

And Georges Goyau (1869-1939), academician and Catholic historian, referring to the white Roman oxen that were washed still whiter in the waters of the Clitunno: "The springs of living water, which on the soil of Umbria Francis placed at the disposition of souls, perform still more marvelous transformations."

That epitomizes "the Franciscan connection" of the Springs and Temple in their evolution from the cult of a pagan river-god through the Early Christian baptism shrine to a truly "Franciscan landscape."

But let us extend Goyau's insight a bit further along the lines of that powerful Early Christian symbolism and art which are so intimately linked with the deeper religious significance of both the Springs and the Temple.

In the pagan era it was cattle and oxen—"Brother Oxen"— that were washed in the clear, cool water of the Springs before being led to march in the triumphal processions of Roman armies toward the temples of the gods. In the Christian era the oxen were "transformed" into sheep and lambs, brethren of the sacrificial Lamb of God who shed his Blood and gave his life for his sheep.

Then the lambs were cleansed of their sin-stains by being immersed in (or sprinkled with) the same limpid stream of "the Jordan of Umbria," in a baptismal bath that permeated their reborn souls with the living waters of the Spirit and Grace of God.

And after that birth into a new inner life and a new outer life style, the lamb-believers were often led in those centuries of persecution—as in many thereafter, including ours—to offer their lives, their all, in the ultimate sacrifice of a baptism of blood. Thus they joined the millenial triumphant procession of that "great multitude which no man can number, from every nation, standing before the Throne and before the Lamb, clothed in white robes, with palm branches in their hands...."

These are they who have come out of the great tribulation. They have washed their robes and made them white in the Blood of the Lamb. . . . They shall thirst no more . . . for the Lamb will guide them to springs of living water" (Apoc 7:9–17).

Another deeply meaningful symbol, often found on Early Christian churches in Umbria, is beautifully sculpted on the typanum of the Tempietto of the Clitunno: the verdant, flowering Cross of Christ from which grow leaves and tendrils, amid grape vines and clusters. In later medieval art this fruitful symbol evolved into the scriptural Tree of Life (immortality in "eternal life") and the related complex Legend of the Tree which served as the cross on Calvary.

Here too we find the basic Christian theme of victory through overcoming, with flower and fruit in everlasting joy, themes that go to the heart of the spirituality of the Umbrian Saint with five bleeding wounds who overcame and radiated true joy.

So while Edward Hutton reported that on his visit to the Springs of the Clitunno "in vain, in vain I looked for the god Clitumnus and could not find him, though Pliny said he was there," devout and perceptive Christians who have stopped to meditate in that paradise-like park so rich in "authentically religious atmosphere," have looked for the God of St. Francis, as Father Gemelli did, and have found Him there. Because He who made it "for our sake" is indeed speaking to us there in the vibrant, living presence of His Creation and the Beauty with which He endowed it "for our sake."

Part One

Umbria's Early Christians: Martyrs and Apostles A.D. 200–400

V

The Martyrs

Julius Caesar wrote of his conquest of Gaul: *Veni, vidi, vici.* I came, I looked around, I won.

1. The Coming of the Good News

About a hundred years later, after Saints Peter and Paul had died as martyrs in Rome, the inhabitants of Umbria began to hear about persons called "Christians" who were filtering into the Eternal City from Palestine and the East. They were reported to believe that a young Jewish prophet named Jesus of Nazareth had demonstrated that he was God Incarnate by performing miracles and by surviving his execution on the cross by order of the Roman prefect Pontius Pilate. Also that Jesus had proclaimed the inauguration of an inward, other-worldly, severely moral Kingdom motivated by God's love for humanity and our love for him, and had founded a church destined to spread over the entire world, until his predicted Second Coming in glory and majesty.

Gradually this revolutionary message of hope and renewal through inner reform, as recorded in the Gospels and Epistles and as lived by courageous, charitable, and compassionate men and women, penetrated along the Via Flaminia into Umbria during the second and third centuries of our era. Unfortunately we have no reliable documents dealing with the church in Umbria in those years. But that there were a number of martyrs is proved by the chapels and churches that were built where their tortured bodies were buried.

Those first Umbrian Christian martyrs could have paraphrased Caesar's words thus: We came. We saw lost souls. We preached. We loved. We were hated. We suffered for others. We died in pain. And we overcame our enemies, inner and outer. (And we did it without chroniclers, biographers, or other scribblers.)

Later, from the sixth to the twelfth centuries, following a law of church-history writing—hagiography abhors a vacuum—this lack of records resulted in the mass production of a series of mostly fabulous and extravagant Acts, Lives, and Passions of early Umbrian martyr saints. For some unknown reason, no other region in Europe seems to have produced so many fictional accounts of persecutions and deaths by torture of Christian martyrs, often alleged to have been bishops without authentic evidence.

One now famous collection of those unhistorical romances or saints-fiction is that of the Twelve Syrian Saints—later wildly inflated to Three Hundred!—which was probably fabricated in the eighth century by a monk in an abbey near Spoleto. It abounds in anachronisms, chronological impossibilities, and historical contradictions. It sowed prolific weeds of confusion in the early history of Christianity in Umbria even after modern critical research, notably that of Monsignor Francesco Lanzoni (d. 1929), had demonstrated its lack of authenticity. The truth will come out, and historical lies do not pay in the end. He who is the Truth is not honored by fiction claiming to be history. We simply have to find and face the facts—and nonfacts—and get them straight.

However, after we have discarded misinformation, there remains a limited body of genuine data. As Lanzoni wrote, "Christian ideas reached Umbria . . . from Syria, from Palestine, from Jerusalem," and "the normal vehicle of this transmission was the Church of Rome, founded by the Apostle Peter, and the dioceses of Umbria were organized from Rome."

We know that early church leaders and lay persons were persecuted, tortured, and executed in and near Rome, because we have reliable documents concerning them. Similar events undoubtedly took place throughout Central Italy as Christianity spread, though records may be lacking. Authentic evidence of the cult of local martyrs in Assisi, Foligno, and Spoleto appears first in tombs, chapels, and churches, and later in liturgical calendars bearing their names.

Thus near Assisi an ancient church by a bridge over the Tescio River, below the Basilica of St. Francis, honored the spot where St. Victorinus died. And at Costano on the banks of the Chiascio, southwest of the Portiuncola, the earliest martyr of Assisi, St. Rufinus, was buried in a Roman sarcophagus in a rural chapel. The city of Foligno developed around the tomb of the martyred St. Felician. And near Spoleto a church enclosed the tomb of the martyr St. Sabinus. In each case, concrete evidence of the local cult predates by centuries the subsequent more-or-less reliable *legendae* or official biographies.

Now we come to the question which is of special interest to friends of St. Francis: What did he know of the martyr saints of his Valley of Spoleto?

In this connection we must realize that even today and for the last thousand years the inhabitants of Italian towns and villages have nourished a fervent, atavistic devotion to their local saints, especially to their patron saints. Assisi's first two patrons were Rufinus and Victorinus—until Francis and Clare also won that rank. The local cult of the patron saint took on two forms: a general, everyday recourse in prayer, preferably while visiting and touching the saint's tomb; and the annual popular celebration of the feast day (August 11 for Rufinus, June 12 for Victorinus).

It is interesting that there is not a single reference to any early Umbrian saint in the entire corpus of Franciscan sources.

No doubt Francis grew up with some knowledge of their legends recorded in the lectionaries of the cathedral, as narrated by his teachers at the canons' school which he attended at San Giorgio and by preachers on the yearly feast days.

In his youth Francis actually participated in at least one such festival. The Festa of San Vittorino included a kind of mystery drama re-enacting the trial and death of the martyr. And also some communally organized games and dances in which the leader carried a staff; now we know that about the year 1205 that leader "carrying the staff in his hand" (357) was Francis (cf FNV ɪ/1, 168; FNV–E 132).

We know too that he used to go and pray at the tomb of St. Rufinus in the crypt (*confessio*) of that patron-martyr's new Duomo, San Rufino (CA 39).

The fearless faith and heroic endurance of these local, hometown heroes who shed their blood on the soil of the *comune* of Assisi, as Saints Peter and Paul had suffered in Rome, must have had a profound, lifelong spiritual influence on Francis and his spirituality, especially his burning longing to die as a martyr which we will treat in Chapter VIII.

So while granting that much of the detailed information about the martyr-saints of Umbria may not be reliable, the fact that it was generally accepted by his contemporaries requires that we survey it briefly as an essential part of his background.

2 *St. Rufinus, Assisi's First Patron Saint*

Note: To distinguish the Saint from his Cathedral, we use St. Rufinus for him and San Rufino for it.

St. Rufinus was the principal patron saint of Assisi and the titular of its second and dominant cathedral (see its complex history in Chaps. XIX–XXI). The documentary evidence and problems relating to him have been thoroughly studied by Monsignor Aldo Brunacci, Assisi's Diocesan Archivist (see Bibliography).

The author of his Legend, written in the eleventh century, claims that he was a bishop. But two far more reliable documents of that century, the Sermon and Hymn on St. Rufinus by St. Peter Damian (who knew the Legend), refer to him only as martyr and not as bishop.

According to the late Legend, Rufinus and his son, also a priest, were persecuted for their faith in their native Asia Minor, then released after converting the Roman governor by miraculous cures. Already a bishop of a diocese in Pontus there, he moved to Italy, first to the region around Avezzano east of Rome and finally to Assisi, where he preached, was arrested, beaten, cast into a furnace, freed by an angel, and by order of the emperor thrown into the Chiascio River with a heavy stone tied to his neck.

Later the local Christians recovered his body and buried it at Costano by the river, building a church over the tomb. Some centuries later the remains were transferred to San Rufino.

In the eleventh century, with the "invention" (discovery or fabrication—see xx) of his Legend, devotion to the Patron Saint intensified and became entangled over the next two centuries in the bitter rivalry between the old and the new cathedrals, between the bishops down at Santa Maria and the canons up at San Rufino.

When this prolonged conflict, along with others, culminated during the lifetime of St. Francis, it is deeply significant that he, with all the tact and strategy of a saint, succeeded in remaining on friendly terms with both the bishop and the canons.

3 *St. Victorinus*

San Vittorino was considered the second martyr-bishop of Assisi. Again we have the same pattern of evidence: first just a rural
church over his tomb, then a translation of his remains to an
urban church, the Benedictine Abbey of San Pietro; and lastly a
fictional eleventh-century Legend, which describes his behead-
ing by the bridge of San Vittorino over the Tescio River, at the
foot of the western hill on which the Basilica of San Francesco
was built.

After the translation of his body, probably at the end of the
tenth century, the original burial church was abandoned. In the
sixteenth century its stones were used in the construction of the
Basilica of Santa Maria degli Angeli.

In 1954 the remains of St. Victorinus were placed in a handsome Roman sarcophagus and given a position of honor in the
main altar of the splendidly restored Romanesque Church of
San Pietro. (On the stay at that Abbey of the French priest-poet
Louis Le Cardonnel in 1906, see TJA 49.)

VI

St. Felician, First Apostle of Umbria

St. Felician, Patron Saint of Foligno, merits our special attention for four good reasons. His oldest Legend, dating from the sixth or seventh century, while not entirely trustworthy, "yet may be true in its main lines" (Lanzoni). Though not a Bishop of Assisi, he preached there and throughout Umbria, like St. Francis. Just outside Assisi on the way down to San Damiano there is a Chapel of San Feliciano, where he is reported to have given a striking, almost "Franciscan," sermon to the first Christians of Assisi. And lastly because it has been plausibly suggested that he may have been the aged saint who appeared to Brother Elias in 1224 and revealed to him that St. Francis would die two years later.

Though often identified as the first Bishop of Foligno, St. Felician's oldest *Vita* specifies that he was elected Bishop of his native town Forum Flaminii (now San Giovanni Profiamma), a village two miles north of Foligno, but that he died as a martyr near Foligno at the age of ninety-four, having been a bishop for 56 years. It also states that "before him no one was called bishop from the City of Rome on the right and left to the Alps" (i.e., the Apennines). His death is placed under the persecution of the Emperor Decius between 249 and 251 (Feast January 24).

St. Felician evangelized most of that region of Central Italy which we now call "Franciscan Italy"—not just the Valley of Spoleto or Umbria, but also parts of neighboring districts in the

Marches, Tuscany, and Latium. Incidentally, one of his three
extant Legends specifies that he traveled on foot, or as modern
Italians say, *col cavallo di San Francesco,* on the horse of St. Francis: legs and feet.

So of the three great apostles of Umbria in church history, St.
Felician is the first, the pioneer. The other two are Franciscans:
Francis, a thousand years later, and Blessed Leopold of Gaiche
(1732–1815), who made the Hermitage of St. Francis on Monte
Luco (see II.5) his headquarters.

The only incident in the life of St. Felician which is narrated in
some detail took place in Assisi. His preaching there aroused
such bitter opposition among the priests of the several pagan
temples that the Saint was beaten and expelled from the city by
the Roman governor.

What happened then is of major significance for these reasons: literally and symbolically it represents the planting of the
Cross of Christ in Assisi; its account in the longer version is
distinguished by a "Franciscan" simplicity and power; the author
was well acquainted with Assisi; and the site was very familiar to
St. Francis.

Here then is the text, translated from the *Vita Sancti Feliciani*
published in the *Analecta Bollandiana:*

> Then the man of God Bishop Felician remained for
> some days in the territory of Assisi, where it is said
> that he erected a cross as a symbol near an ancient
> mausoleum. And encouraging and blessing his followers, he said: "Act manfully in the Lord, and
> strengthen one another, and let all your belongings
> be held in common. The threats of wicked highpriests vanish and must be accounted as dung. For
> those men will perish in the world to come, but you
> will have eternal life after death. One thing I urge
> upon you, very dear brethren: that you strive to re-

vere and love the cross which I have fixed in the ground as the Way in honor of our Lord Jesus Christ. And pray to God the Creator there on your knees in the evening, morning, and at noon, and take care to offer Him your petitions and praise."

Hence in that same place until this very day the Lord has deigned to manifest many marvels through the intercession of Blessed Felician, Martyr and Bishop; that is, his words have been confirmed: persons possessed by demons have been cured, those suffering from leprosy have been cleansed, those afflicted with palsy and fever have recovered their health, and damaging tempests have been averted, and twofold good things have been the lot of those dwelling in that place, both those in times past and those who are now prospering there today.

This is one of the most striking texts in the often insipid or fantastic literature on early Umbrian saints. It has the qualities of superior hagiography: directness, conciseness, sincerity, and vigor. It is also rich in factual information of importance to the local history of Assisi. Scholars should try to solve the problem of its approximate date, which the Bollandist editor left open.

Several points are worth noting. For instance, the stress on acting "manfully" and strengthening one another, with scorn for the pagan priests. The bishop's rather surprising recommendation of a revival of the famous "all things in common" of the first Christians in Jerusalem (from Acts 2:44 and 4:32) would seem to link apostolic times with the medieval monastic and lay poverty movements . . . and St. Francis.

Noteworthy from the point of view of spirituality and liturgical prayer is the cult of the cross as "the Way" (*trames*), with a kind of lay office of praise and petition to be recited kneeling thrice daily.

Also of interest is the reference to the "ancient mausoleum," as that is the Tomb of the Roman poet Propertius (see III.1).

Lastly there is the valuable information that describes a popular local shrine, with cult and cures at the site, enduring from the third century and still potent centuries later. Hence this spot is obviously of importance in the Early Christian and medieval history of Assisi.

Moreover it has a threefold link with St. Francis.

The whole slope below the city toward San Damiano was known as the Colle di San Feliciano. And Francis passed by the Chapel of San Feliciano—perhaps with a prayer to the "man of God"—whenever he went from Assisi to San Damiano or back; also when as a boy he went with his father to some of the latter's fields on the plain below San Damiano; and likewise later when he went to or from the Chapel of San Pietro della Spina near those fields, which he repaired after San Damiano (FNV-E 248).

The Hill or Chapel of San Feliciano is mentioned in archival documents of 1065, 1091, 1141, etc. In 1198 the Chapel belonged to the bishop, but by 1217 it had become a dependency of the canons of San Rufino, as it remains to this day. Built perhaps as early as the fourth century, it is a small, unpretentious, roughly square stone structure.

In our times the Chapel had fallen into a state of delapidation perhaps resembling that of San Damiano before St. Francis repaired it. In this case it was an American woman who undertook the restoration of San Felicianuccio, as it is called in Assisi. She was Mary (Molly) Emlen Lowell, born in 1884 in the well-known Bostonian family. Her first husband was a Philadelphian, Frank Lloyd; they had a son of the same name. In 1942 she married the eighth Earl of Berkeley and became a British citizen. Originally an Episcopalian, she joined the Roman Catholic Church and lived for many years in Assisi, where she died on August 12, 1975. The funeral Mass was offered by her American friend, Father Salvator Butler, O.F.M., of San Damiano (to whom we are endebted for this information).

In the 1920s she began the restoration of the Chapel of St.

Felician in thanksgiving to the Blessed Mother for the cure of her son from rheumatic fever. The work advanced slowly over the decades until her last years. She herself painted five mural panels behind the altar depicting Mary and the Christ Child with St. Francis and his first friars. Lady Berkeley liked to go with friends to the Chapel for Mass or Benediction of the Blessed Sacrament, celebrated in recent years by Father Salvator.

Thus in this century the memory of St. Felician, Umbria's first apostle, has been honored by two American disciples of St. Francis . . . and commemorated in this book by a third.

VII

St. Francis and St. Felician

The several links between the first and the second great Apostles of Umbria may at first seem somewhat indirect, yet they exist, and they will appear more substantial as we outline them.

We have already noted the principal one: both Saints evangelized Umbria and its neighboring districts. Felician planted Christianity there, and Francis revived it. Both lived and loved and preached the same "Way," the Cross of Christ.

Second, the fact that San Damiano is located squarely on the Hill of St. Felician and that the latter's Chapel actually was close to San Damiano is surely of more than superficial significance when viewed in the light of faith and Providence. Right there on the same hillside where the Martyr and first Apostle erected the cross and urged Assisi's first Christians to revere it and pray before it, a millenium later Jesus Christ Himself animated the beautiful painted Crucifix of San Damiano and told young Francis to "repair My House," that House of God in Assisi and Umbria which the martyrs had founded, because it was "completely destroyed" (see TJA 159). And Francis repaired it by renewing and spreading the faith and ethics and life style of the early Christians, "the Way" of loving prayer and courage and brotherhood and sacrifice which St. Felician had first preached and planted there. On "the Way" of Christ on the spirituality of St. Francis, see Esser in Bibliography, Part Two, (3).

Were the two Saints really dissimilar because Felician was a martyr and Francis was not, technically? Well, the Little Poor Man of Assisi was a martyr in desire and a martyr of pain with his five bleeding wounds. This essential aspect of his life and spirituality is so important that it will be surveyed separately in the next Chapter.

The most direct link, potentially, between Felician of Foligno and Francis of Assisi lies in the possibility, which may even be a plausible probability, that St. Felician was the unnamed elderly priest who appeared in a vision to Brother Elias in Foligno in the summer of 1224 and informed him that Francis had only two more years to live. Here is the principal source of that incident (1C 109):

> When the Blessed Father himself and Brother Elias were once staying in Foligno, one night when they had fallen asleep, a certain priest dressed in white, very old and advanced in age, of venerable appearance, stood before Brother Elias and said: "Arise, Brother, and tell Brother Francis that eighteen years have passed since he renounced the world and adhered to Christ, and remaining in this life only two years from now, he will enter into the way of all flesh, the Lord calling him to Himself."

This important episode in the life of St. Francis—especially in his inner life—has only been studied once, in an article by the great church historian of Foligno Monsignor Michele Faloci Pulignani (d. 1940). With pardonable *campanilismo* (pride in the local church) yet with plausible reasoning, he suggested that the elderly priest in the vision was none other than St. Felician, the Patron-Protector of Foligno, whom he also considered (erroneously) its first bishop. His two main reasons were the "advanced age" of the "very old" priest, for the Martyr was ninety-four when he died, and second, the place itself, the city of Foligno, where the site of the Apostle's tomb, selected by himself, evolved into a major church and shrine and eventually into the duomo or cathedral.

A more subtle yet equally compelling connection may be found in two more links with Francis that are perhaps involved in the reference to his renouncing the world eighteen years earlier. Could this recall not only the Message of the Crucifix in San Damiano near St. Felician's Chapel on his Hill in Assisi, but also Francis' unforgettable visit on that same day to Foligno to sell the cloth and horse? Perhaps while there Francis may have prayed at the Martyr's Tomb in the Cathedral of San Feliciano, before hiking back to begin his new life of adherence to Christ on the Hill of St. Felician.

Incidentally, the handsome Romanesque façade of Foligno's Duomo is dated 1133, but the front of the enlarged left transept or second façade was built in 1201. Still more incidentally the Cathedral contains a large marble plaque on which is inscribed a Latin hymn in honor of St. Felician written by the Bishop of Perugia from 1846 to 1877 who belonged to the Third Order of St. Francis and who "repaired" the Roman Catholic House of God as Pope Leo XIII from 1878 to 1903.

So in effect St. Francis of Assisi, being destined to become St. Felician's successor as second great Apostle of Umbria, began his new life in Christ by going from the Hill of St. Felician to the Civitas Sancti Feliciani (as the Duomo area of Foligno was still called in the twelfth century) and then back to the Colle di San Feliciano outside Assisi, where the Martyr had first planted the Cross of Christ and where Jesus on the Crucifix of San Damiano spoke to Francis a millenium later. You must agree that there seems to be in all this a meaningful, mystical Providence.

This circumstantial evidence therefore strongly suggests that Brother Elias' elderly priest was St. Felician. Neither Elias nor

Francis ventured to name him, presumably because he did not
identify himself. We can only wonder why he appeared to the
very practical nonmystic Elias instead of directly to Francis.
Perhaps in order that the vision should be authoritatively reported by its recipient soon after the Saint's death to Friar
Thomas of Celano who recorded it in his First Life in 1229.

Very significant also is the fact that Francis himself testified to
the profound effect which the vision and prophecy had on his
inner life during the remaining two years of his life. He reminded Elias of it while lying ill in the Vescovado a few weeks
before he died, saying:

> Do you remember when you saw that vision in
> Foligno and you told me someone said to you that I
> was going to live only two years more? Before you saw
> that vision, by the grace of the Holy Spirit which
> suggests and puts all good in the heart and in the
> mouth of His faithful, I used to think about my end
> often day and night, but from that hour when you
> saw the vision, every day I have been more intent on
> thinking about the day of death. (CA 64. SP 121)

Now it is well known that many Saints have been forewarned
of the time, often the very hour, of their approaching death.
Few, however, seem to have had two full years in which to pre-
pare their souls for that blessed day of liberation and reward
which the Church aptly calls their Nativity . . . in Heaven. Such
was the exceptional grace provided on that night in Foligno
apparently by St. Felician to St. Francis.

A minor puzzle concerning the vision in Foligno is the
chronological question: did it occur before or after the forty-day
retreat of Francis at La Verna during which he received the
stigmata? In other words, was the vision around August 1 or on
his return to the Valley of Spoleto in mid-November, 1224? The
explicit expression "two years more" seems to favor July or Au-

gust rather than November, as Francis died on October 3 (see discussion in EBB 390-91).

More information on the church history of Foligno, general and Franciscan, will be found in the remarkably dramatic life of its little-known Bishop Bonfil (d. 1115), another great contemplative—monk, bishop, Holy Land pilgrim, and hermit—which will be sketched in *Forefathers of St. Francis.*

VIII

St. Francis and the Martyrs

None of the few references to martyrs in the recorded words of St. Francis applies directly to the Early Christian martyrs, either of Rome or Umbria. It is striking that when he touched on the subject, he had in mind later or contemporary examples: Charlemagne and Roland, and his own friars who died for their faith in Morocco. In both instances he reproved those who sought glory-by-association in celebrating or merely recounting such heroes' deeds.

When he heard of the deaths of the first Franciscan martyrs in North Africa, in 1220, he exclaimed: "Now I can truly say that I have five Friars Minor!" Then, seeing the pride which his companions were taking in listening to the *Passio* or written report of the five martyrs' sufferings and death, and also hearing in it some words praising himself, he had the reading stopped and forbade its being read again, saying: "Let everyone glory in his own martyrdom and not in that of others!" (Jordan of Giano's *Chronicle,* 8).

However, his close early companion Blessed Brother Giles of Assisi once spontaneously composed a beautiful short poem, which his intimate friend Brother Gratian interpreted as applying to "the Apostles and Martyrs," i.e., the Early Christian martyrs. Of course the idea and the words are Giles' own, and he was a perfect example of a very "original character." But it is quite

likely that his poem reflected a general concept of the Early
Christian martyrs which he derived from and shared with Francis.

The gist of the poem (text in TJA 199) is a simple, lyrical
prayer that God's Love might make of him a castle or small town
not built with stone or iron or wood. Now Giles recited it with
great fervor to five superiors of the Order who came to visit him
at his hermitage of Monteripido outside Perugia. This is how
Gratian interpreted for them Giles' symbolism: "Those castles
and towns were the Holy Apostles and Martyrs who were supremely brave and victorious without weapons made of iron or
any other temporal support" (AF 3. 101). The key Latin word
adminiculum means support, aid, instrument. This phrase clearly
had a powerful thrust, especially when addressed to superiors of
a religious order or church officials: pray for the grace of being
strong and overcoming *without temporal support*.

As to the Franciscan Order, Giles was evidently "giving a message" to its superiors at a time—around 1250—when it was already suffering from the conflict over poverty which was to
afflict and divide it for the next hundred years and
more . . . until Blessed Paolo dei Trinci of Foligno founded the
Observant reform by a return to the *ritiri* and to the original
ideal of an absolute minimum of temporal support, with a
maximum of faith and prayer, especially contemplative prayer.

That this concept as expressed by Giles and Gratian can be
traced to Francis himself can be shown by many of his statements
on poverty, but perhaps most decisively and directly by one of
the most amazingly frank and forceful declarations he ever
made, in the very first year of the Order and to his own ecclesiastical superior, the contentious Bishop Guido of Assisi.

When the begging of the first few companions aroused scorn
and opposition, the Bishop summoned Francis, who frequently
consulted him, and said: "Your life seems very hard and severe
to me—that is, to possess nothing in this world." And here is the

fearless, lapidary reply of the Little Poor Man: "*My Lord, if we had possessions, it would be necessary for us to have weapons to protect them, because conflicts and lawsuits arise therefrom, and as a result the love of God and neighbor is impeded in many ways. And on that account we do not want to possess anything temporal in this world*" (3S 35. AF 3. 675. AP 17. Not in 1C, 2C, B).

We sorely need an in-depth study of Guido as man and as bishop and as Francis' bishop. Here as background for those absolutely basic words of the Saint which might well be called his *magna carta,* we shall only note these facts. Guido himself, on being reconciled with the mayor by the Canticle in 1225, publicly admitted something that everyone in Assisi knew very well: "By nature I quickly become angry" (CA 44. SP 101). And that nature of his, which Fortini describes as "greedy . . . proud . . . imperious . . . haughty . . . violent," embroiled him in over half a dozen "conflicts and lawsuits" arising, as Francis boldly told him, from "possessions," i.e., property rights, and resulting in "impeding love of God and neighbor in many ways." We will have to return to this *magna carta* of St. Francis when we consider his cult of poverty as a deliberate reaction to the temporal wealth of the medieval dioceses and abbeys—to say nothing of his own father's (see Chap. XVIII).

It is therefore evident that the "weapons" and "temporal support" of Giles and Gratian can be traced right back to Francis' *arma* and *aliquid temporale.* Moreover, Giles as third companion had heard Francis tell the first companions what he said to the Bishop. Consequently, we can conclude that the Poverello's concept of poverty was directly connected with his concept of the spirituality and way of life of the Early Christian martyrs and bishops. In other words Francis urged Bishop Guido to be more like St. Felician. Let us express the hope that this important subject will receive the full study which it requires but has not had.

We know that St. Francis burned intensely with the desire to imitate both Christ and the early martyrs not only in renouncing possessions but above all in shedding his blood for the faith, for conversions. In fact, he deliberately sought martyrdom among the Moslems no less than three times. But Providence gave him instead the pain and bleeding of the stigmata which he endured for two long, active years. And those sufferings were generally considered equivalent to martyrdom (see 1C 55–57. 2C 210–13. B 9.5–9. B 13.2). He himself testified during the agony of his last days at the Portiuncola: "To suffer this illness for three days would be more painful for me than to exchange it for any kind of martyrdom—I do not mean regarding the reward, but only as to the suffering from pain" (1C 107).

We should note that most of the Saints commemorated in the papal curia breviary adopted by St. Francis for his Order were martyrs, though none were Umbrian, except for locally added entries for Rufinus. Thus the lives and passions of the martyrs which he read in the breviary nocturns were almost all those of Rome and the Christian East. While some of those documents have been shown to be unreliable by modern research, others are historically authentic, for example the Acts of Saints Perpetua and Felicity (March 6). In all cases those Saints were "supremely brave and victorious without weapons and temporal support."

That was the ideal which St. Francis learned from their example and lived and revived by his own example, thus transmitting it to thousands of his followers down the centuries, sowing the martyr seed of Christians and repairing the House of the Crucified Savior, the model of Christian martyrs, past, present, and future.

St. Bonaventure developed a striking theology of martyrdom on Franciscan lines which has been admirably outlined by E. Randolph Daniel in the two excellent studies listed in the Bibliography. As an appendix to this Chapter I would also urge the reader to consult the rich article on "Martyre" in the *Dictionnaire de spiritualité* (DS 10:718-737), especially its Part II on "Théologie et spiritualité du martyr" (726-32).

As a concluding footnote on the Christian martyrs of Umbria, we may note that Todi was the birthplace of the last Pope honored in the Church as a martyr: Pope St. Martin I, who died in prison in the Crimea in 656 for having condemned the Greek Emperor's defense of monothelitism (denying the two wills of Christ, human and divine); see his eloquent and pathetic letter from exile and prison in BTA 4.320.

IX

The Founding Fathers

A young man or woman of Assisi who was converted to Christianity at the age of twenty by the preaching of St. Felician about A.D. 250, just before he died, could have lived to see the day in 313 when the Emperior Constantine's Edict of Milan granted official toleration to the Church—if he or she survived the last great persecution under Diocletian in 304.

By then Italy counted over 300 known martyrs. Their sacrificial deaths were the foundation stones of the new House of God. Its founding fathers were the bishops, its master builders, who laid its spiritual and material foundations in the fourth century. A Roman synod in 250 was attended by sixty bishops. By the year 600, Italy had over two hundred.

1 *The First Churches*

In Umbria the fourth century was relatively calm and serene, though reliable records of individual bishops do not appear until the end of the century. However, the enduring memorials left by the emerging Christian communities were their first church buildings, five of which are still standing.

One of the earliest and most striking, as we have seen (in IV.4) is the small Temple of the Clitunno. Also dating from the fourth or fifth centuries are the two remarkable circular churches of

Sant'Angelo in Perugia and San Salvatore in Terni. The former is larger, resembling Rome's Pantheon, ringed by eighteen Corinthian columns. It has been suggested that it may have been a replica of the Constantinian Anastasis Basilica over the Holy Sepulcher of Christ in Jerusalem, similar to one in Antioch and to San Stefano Rotondo in Rome (built in 468). Of special liturgical interest is the fact that such round churches were designed for penitential processions.

Spoleto, being already a major political and cultural center, has two Early Christian basilicas of the same period, both outside the city: San Salvatore on the north and San Pietro to the south. The former, restored in 875 and transformed in the twelfth century, has Syrian motives in its oldest elements. The magnificent sculptures on the façade of the latter, which have rightly been called "the masterpiece of medieval sculpture in Umbria," were added in the twelfth century.

The spiritual importance of these Early Christian churches in Umbria has been stressed by an art historian, Guglielmo De Angelis D'Ossat: "These monumental buildings attest to the flowering and expansion of a Christian life in associative forms, which we know from various sources was alive in Umbria. They confirm the sudden surging of that mystical spirituality which distinguishes Umbria" (PUU 253). Other scholars have also noted that for various reasons the message of the Gospel seems to have found an especially fertile soil in the souls of the people of Umbria.

2 The First Bishops

Spoleto also has the honor of being the see of the two earliest Umbrian bishops or founding fathers of the post persecution era of whose identity and activities we have reliable evidence. They were Bishops Spes and Achilleus, and they governed the diocese successively from about 380 until after 420, the first for thirty-two years. Like St. Francis, both composed religious poems, though in elegant Latin verses.

Bishop Spes followed the example of his contemporary Pope Damasus in writing a poem in honor of a local martyr. He also discovered the body of a martyr (as did St. Ambrose, another contemporary). And he prepared his own tomb in the Church of the Holy Apostles.

Bishop Achilleus, like St. Francis, had a special devotion to St. Peter, and he brought to Spoleto from Rome a section of Peter's chains for the large Church of San Pietro which he erected outside the city, at the foot of Monte Luco. That church became the traditional burial site of his successors. But it was never the cathedral, as stated in some guidebooks. Many of the first Italian cathedrals were suburban, i.e., outside the original city walls.

Bishop Achilleus celebrated the primacy of St. Peter in several eloquent Latin poems, stressing the Apostle's prerogative of loosing souls from the chains of sin, and thus he promoted veneration of the section of the actual chains. In 419 he was chosen by the Imperial Court in Ravenna to administer baptism to converts in the Lateran Basilica in Rome on Holy Saturday. In a report from Rome to Ravenna he was referred to as *sanctus Achilleus episcopus.*

A third Umbrian bishop of this period earned a notable place in church history. Bishop Decentius of Gubbio submitted eight liturgical questions to the Holy See in 416, and received from Pope St. Innocent I a full decretal reply which constitutes a primary document in the history of the liturgy.

Calling for uniformity among the churches in the West founded by priests sent out by St. Peter and his successors, the Pope noted that while Decentius was familiar with the liturgical usages of Rome, the reply would treat the eight questions for the benefit of other bishops so that they could correct deviations or innovations.

Among the specific points at issue were the following. Just when in the Mass should the Pax be given, i.e., before or after the Consecration—answer: after, but before Communion. When should the diptych be read—during the Canon. Could confirmation be given by priests—no, only by the bishop. When were penitents to be reconciled—on Holy Thursday. Was Saturday as well as Friday a day of fast—yes, because the Apostles mourned on Holy Saturday.

The Pope's letter also throws important light indirectly on conditions in the small Umbrian Diocese of Gubbio, Assisi's neighbor to the north. A passing reference to Bishop Decentius' "predecessors" shows that the see's origin extends back into the fourth century, though he is its first reliably documented ordinary. The letter implies that the Christian community of Gubbio was in a state of placid normalcy, as it mentions no doctrinal disputes or moral disorders or drastic innovations. References to rural churches indicate that Christianity was spreading from the urban population into the countryside among the *pagani,* the peasants, who would soon form the backbone of the Church.

Gubbio is an example of a town which, for defense against marauding armies, was moved from the plain to the slope of an adjacent hill during the later period of the barbarian invasions, whereas Foligno and Spoleto remained on the plain, and Assisi and Perugia were founded on hillsides.

Still regarding Gubbio, looking ahead we may note in passing that after the founding around the year 1000 of the Hermitage of the Holy Cross at Fonte Avellana in the mountains north of Gubbio, made famous by its great Prior St. Peter Damian and by Dante (see TJA 219), at least seven of its monks became bishops of Gubbio. Among them was Blessed Villano (d. 1239) who was known as "Father of the Poor" and who was a close friend of St. Francis.

Gubbio's greatest son was its Patron Saint, Bishop Ubaldo (d. 1160), a model contemplative and reformer, who was canonized in 1192 when Francis was ten years old. Both Saints Peter Damian and Ubaldo will be treated at length as prayerful "repairers" of God's House in Umbria in *Forefathers of St. Francis.*

One more enduring relic of the Early Christian culture of the Umbrian church in the era of the founding fathers must be mentioned because of its intrinsic importance and because of an indirect Franciscan connection.

This is the first-rate sculptural art found on several outstanding late classical and Early Christian sarcophagi or large, ornate stone coffins. Two fine examples can be seen today, one in the crypt of San Rufino in Assisi, where St. Francis often prayed. It contains the remains of Assisi's martyr St. Rufinus, and is a pagan work of about A.D. 200 depicting in relief scenes from the romantic myth of Diana and Endymion. Its dramatic part in the conflict between the old and new cathedral in the eleventh century will be narrated in Chapter XIX, thanks to St. Peter Damian's invaluable contemporary account.

The second sarcophagus, dating from around the year 360, was used in Perugia in 1262 as a profoundly appropriate tomb for the body of St. Francis' third companion, that great contemplative and early Franciscan mystic, Blessed Brother Giles of Assisi. It is now on display in the beautiful little Oratorio of San Bernardino in Perugia.

On this masterpiece of Early Christian art are represented seven figures between eight columns. Seated in the center is a youthful yet mature Christ the Teacher, with a feminine person on his right probably symbolic of Mother Church. The other five figures are Apostles. Two upper sections show Noah in the ark and Jonah and the whale.

Providence and the people of Perugia chose this handsome sarcophagus as a fitting funeral monument for the humble and prayerful Brother Giles whose life, prayers, and "golden words" perfectly exemplified the basic Franciscan vocation and charism of repairing God's House by humility and poverty and Francis' contemplative "spirit of prayer and devotion."

For Blessed Brother Giles himself was made by Jesus, whom he called in his poem "my beautiful Brother Love," into that "castle that has no stone or iron or wood" of which he sang (see VIII): one of "the apostles who were supremely brave and strong and victorious without iron weapons or any other temporal support." So it was deeply fitting that his body be entombed in a splendid work of art of the century in which Mother Church gained that freedom for growth which the supremely strong and brave martyrs and apostles had victoriously won for her by their sacrificial sufferings and deaths, their Christ-like "passions."

Incidentally, regarding tombs, Umbria's first Christians dug out one—but apparently only one—catacomb cemetery like those around Rome, located near the Via Flaminia between Todi and Carsulae.

Insofar as relative calm prevailed in Umbria during the gradual decline and fall of the decadent Roman Empire, it was the calm before the storm of the barbarian invasions, or the twilight before the murky Dark Ages ahead.

Part Two

Umbria's Dark Ages
400—1000

X

The Barbarian Invaders

Geopolitics abhors a vacuum. Rome's decline created a vacuum throughout Italy. For 550 years—between 410 and 962—Umbria, being in the center of that vacuum, suffered no less than eight major and minor invasions. Most of the invaders were Germanic in stock, and they came from the north, down the Via Flaminia.

For the record, here is a brief list. In 410 Alaric's Goths sacked Rome. In 452 Attila the Hun threatened but did not reach Rome. But Genseric's Vandals did in 455. From 493 to 555 the Ostrogoth Kingdom ruled Central Italy. But between 404 and about 750 the Byzantine Eastern Roman Empire maintained a subcapital in Ravenna and therefore had to keep open a communications corridor with Rome that ran through Gubbio and Perugia. From 568 to 774 the Germanic Lombards ruled the Duchy of Spoleto (including Assisi). Then, after 774, Charlemagne's Franks occupied much of Italy. But a new vacuum arose after the division of his Empire into French and German halves in 870. In 881 Saracens invaded parts of Central Italy and Hungarians in 915 and 924. Finally most of Italy was united to Germany in 962 when Otto I was crowned Emperor of Rome.

Throughout these "dark ages" the only effective governing power in many Italian towns was, by default, that of the local bishop. And in the region around Rome, even before the passing of its last emperor in 476, the principal authority, spiritual and hence also temporal, was that of the popes, especially when they were outstanding leaders like Saints Leo the Great (440–461) and Gregory the Great (590–604).

The process by which the bishops of Italy found themselves obliged to serve their people both as spiritual shepherds and temporal rulers is of profound significance in the evolution of the local churches.

First, the new cathedrals which arose within the city walls became centers of social as well as religious activities. The bishop directed such charitable undertakings as assistance to the sick and the poor and pilgrims. Gradually he earned official recognition by civil officials and laws. His election by clergy and laity made him the representative and protector of the entire community. Eventually he came to be known in many cases as the *defensor civitatis,* a formal title originally assigned to a civic officer whose duty was to protect citizens from dishonest prices and taxes.

Hence the bishop organized his espiscopal court and often served on important civic or royal commissions. His administration extended into rural areas and even, during vacancies, into adjoining dioceses. In nearby Umbria, he was under the direct jurisdiction of the pope and curia in Rome, which he visited more frequently than remoter bishops.

Assisi appears in historical records for the first time after the Roman era during the war between the Byzantine Empire and the Ostrogoths in the sixth century. Two notable events in its history took place around 545: it was besieged and captured, and its bishop was selected for an important diplomatic mission. A brief survey of these incidents will throw light on the general conditions of the church and people in Umbria in that century which covers the lifetimes of St. Benedict, who was born at Norcia in Umbria and died about 546, and St. Gregory the Great (d. 604).

By this time the power and integrity of Roman civilization had fallen to the point where several of the so-called "barbarian" rulers actually introduced much needed law and order. That is what the Ostrogoth King Theodoric the Great (493–526) did in Umbria. Besides building a palace in Spoleto, he drained the marshy *lacus Umber,* the lake on the plain between Assisi and Bettona (see iv.3).

After Theodoric's death in Ravenna, the ambitious Byzantine Emperor Justinian the Great (527–565) strove to retake Italy from the Goths. The resulting Gothic Wars devastated Central Italy during the next twenty-five years, and city after city suffered repeated sieges and sackings. Spoleto, for example, changed hands four times in the eight years, 545 to 552.

In those years the two military opponents fighting across Umbria presented a sharp contrast. The Byzantine general was an Armenian eunuch named Narses, while the Gothic King was the famous Totila, whom the historian Edward Gibbon praised as chaste and temperate, liberal and courteous, dependable and merciful. He was finally defeated and died after a decisive battle near Gualdo on the Flaminia in 552.

But first, in the years 545–548, Assisi, Perugia, and Gubbio underwent the horrors of siege and capture, and in all three their bishops played prominent roles.

The Byzantine captain defending Assisi refused to yield the relatively unfortified city and fought valiantly until killed. In 547 Totila chose Bishop Aventius of Assisi as his legate on an embassy to the Emperor Justinian in Constantinople. Unfortunately we have no other information about this first authentically documented Bishop of Assisi. But his selection as special envoy indicates that in those years of conflict the local bishops were looked upon by both Goths and Byzantines as key representatives of Italy's urban populations.

The fate of Perugia's Bishop Erculanus was tragically different. When the strongly fortified town was captured in 547, after a seven-year siege and prolonged famine, he was executed for having fearlessly sustained his fellow-citizens' resistance. The people of Perugia have ever since considered Bishop Ercolano as their major hero and patron.

Gubbio, as an ally of Perugia, was also besieged, taken, and destroyed, and its bishop and foremost citizens were put to death, according to local tradition. Narses is reported to have had it rebuilt on the adjoining hillside.

The effects of the Gothic Wars on Umbria—and Rome—were disastrous. Owing to the province's strategic location along the Via Flaminia, successive waves of Goths and Byzantines despoiled the towns and countryside, causing famines, pestilences, and rural depopulation.

By the year 600, Italy had entered the murky tunnel of the Dark Ages which were to last another four long centuries. But first, from 590 to 604, one of the brightest lights in the entire history of Christianity radiated a brilliant and beneficent radiance from Rome throughout Europe. This was Pope St. Gregory the Great, perhaps the greatest of all St. Peter's successors and the founder of the culture of the Middle Ages which was still vigorous in Umbria during the lifetime of St. Francis six centuries later.

XI

St. Gregory the Great and the Goths in Umbria

The bishops of Umbria lived and worked in a specially close relationship with the Holy See in Rome, only a hundred miles to the south. Hence the history of the church in Umbria is intimately linked with that of the papacy, both directly through immediate administrative jurisdiction and also indirectly through spiritual, liturgical, and cultural influences.

Consequently the figures of the two founding fathers of Christian Rome, Saints Peter and Paul, together with several outstanding successors of Peter as popes, loomed in the eyes of the Christians of neighboring Umbria as heroes of gigantic and almost legendary stature.

The first of such figures was St. Sylvester I, who governed the Church from 314 to 335, in the first two decades of its liberation. The dramatic legends which soon clustered around the image of this Pope Sylvester, such as his healing and baptizing the Emperor Constantine, were vividly depicted in splendid thirteenth-century paintings in the Church of the Santi Quattro Coronati in Rome (where Brother Giles lodged, because its monks were from the Abbey of Sassovivo near Foligno). It was Pope Sylvester who made the Lateran Basilica Rome's cathedral and who built, with the Emperor's help, the major churches of St. Peter, Santa Croce, and St. Lawrence beyond the Walls.

The second figure of heroic stature among the popes of this

era was St. Leo the Great (440–461), whose firm, clear-sighted, and forceful sanctity impressed even Attila the Hun at their encounter in northern Italy in 452 when the Pope persuaded him not to attack Rome. However, three years later, Leo was only able to dissuade the Vandal chief Genseric from burning the city, but not from pillaging it for a fortnight.

St. Gregory the Great was a practical Roman nobleman-statesman who became a monk and a mystic and then ably served for thirteen fruitful years as "the Servant of the Servants of God." He was the first to adopt that title, which perfectly characterized him.

This giant among men and among men of God is a figure of profound importance for students of St. Francis because in the early thirteenth century many of Gregory's powerful writings were still popular, formative religious materials. Also for several other reasons, such as his relations with the church in Umbria and the enduring elements of his contemplative-active spirituality. We will defer a study of the striking common themes of his spirituality and that of St. Francis to the sequel of this book, *Forefathers of St. Francis.*

Moreover, besides being the original biographer of that great Umbrian St. Benedict, Gregory also included in his widely read *Dialogues* valuable accounts of various Umbrian monks and hermits and bishops of the sixth century, including St. Isaac of Spoleto, the Syrian founder of the hermitages on Monte Luco (see II.5). In his many visits to monasteries and cathedrals, the Poverello must have heard parts of the works of St. Gregory read aloud, in addition to those which he found in his breviary.

The Dialogues are rich in human-interest anecdotes concerning saintly bishops, priests, and monks in Italy during the sixth century. Although they do not refer to Assisi, they contain data on bishops of five towns in Umbria.

The basic theme of the first three Books of *The Dialogues* is that Italy too had in recent times "persons whose lives give evidence of extraordinary spiritual powers . . . signs or miracles." A secondary theme is that through those saints God often humbled the fierce Goths and Lombards. The Fourth Book narrates marvels, visions, and prophecies which demonstrate the survival of the soul after the death of the body. The Second Book is a popular life of St. Benedict stressing his miracles.

Gibbon's portrait of King Totila the Goth as a just and merciful man differs sharply from his image in *The Dialogues,* which call him "crafty . . . cruel . . . utterly heartless." St. Benedict is quoted as rebuking him for his "crimes," saying: "You are the cause of many evils. Put an end to your wickedness." And in fact, after their dramatic encounter in 543, during the nine years which the Saint foretold that the King would still live, Totila "was less cruel" (Book II.15).

Yet it was after that meeting that Totila executed Bishop Erculanus of Perugia in 547. In western Tuscany the King gave orders that Bishop Cerbonius be clawed to death by a ferocious bear, but "the brute beast acted with an almost human heart" and humbly licked the feet and hands of the bishop. Reacting to the cheers of the crowd, Totila was moved to honor the saint and "imitate the meekness of the bear" (Book III.11).

At Otricoli near Orte in the southern tip of Umbria, Totila "in a burst of rage" had Bishop Fulgentius arrested, but "his harsh attitude was changed into one of great respect" when he heard that the prelate remained completely dry while standing outdoors in a severe thunderstorm (Book III.12). No wonder that Gregory, who was about twelve when the King of the Goths died, later called those times "the terrible days of King Totila the heretic" (Book III.13).

Another Umbrian bishop, St. Cassius of Narni, inspired great esteem in the Gothic ruler. Totila attributed the bishop's unusually reddish complexion to alcoholism, until the Saint freed the king's sword-bearer from diabolic obsession in the presence of the whole army (Book III.6). *The Dialogues* also mention a Bishop Probus of Rieti who was visited by several martyrs in radiant white robes just before he died (Book IV.13). St. Gregory's accounts of Umbrian monks and hermits will be treated in *Forefathers*.

The heroic figure of St. Benedict emerges in *The Dialogues* with profound significance. We may note especially those qualities of personality and spirituality which he shared with both Gregory and Francis: practicality combined with mysticism, keen psychological insight and realism, masterful gifts as a leader of men, and above all a firm stress on the primary value of the mixed life of prayer (first) and action (almost equally vital).

XII

The Lombard Dukes of Spoleto

During the two hundred years between 569 and 773, Assisi was part of the Lombard Duchy of Spoleto. Though no longer ruled by the Lombards, the Duchy survived until taken into the States of the Church in 1198 by Pope Innocent III.

It was the destiny of Central Italy during the early and high Middle Ages to be occupied and ruled by four successive waves of foreigners from the north: the Goths in the sixth century, the Lombards in the seventh and eighth, the Franks in the ninth, and the Swabian Hohenstaufens in the eleventh and twelfth centuries.

The Lombard era was of decisive importance for Umbria and Assisi because it marked the end of the struggle for mastery between the Byzantine emperors and the Germanic rulers, and because the strategically located Duchy finally was aligned with Rome and the papacy. For the church in Umbria this period was one of persecution at first, as the Lombards were Arians (denying the equality of the Son with the Father), then one of confusion and consolidation while they gradually accepted Catholicism and turned to Rome.

Again St. Gregory the Great is a valuable witness, for he lived under both Goths and Lombards. About twelve when Totila died in 552, he was about thirty when the Lombards established their Duchies of Spoleto to the north and Benevento to the south of Rome. The capital of the Lombard Kingdom was Pavia near Milan, in Lombardy. During his thirteen years reign as pope, Gregory had to protect the Church and its people and lands from the aggressive Lombard kings and dukes and their Arian clergy. His *Dialogues* and numerous Letters provide a vivid picture of the problems facing the Church in those years.

"Wild hordes of Lombards descended on us," he wrote. "Cities were sacked, forts overthrown, churches burned, monasteries and cloisters destroyed" (Book III.38). "They are a cruel people" (Book III.37).

However, it is noteworthy that unlike the Goths, the Lombards seem to have refrained from making martyrs of local bishops. Yet St. Gregory recorded many cases of executions of priests, deacons, and monks, as well as laymen. Of the Arian clergy he commented: "God keeps a check on the fury of the Lombards by not allowing their unholy priests, who look upon themselves as directors of our people, to attack the faith of the orthodox Christians. This is what they have repeatedly tried to do . . . but some marvel from heaven has always opposed them" (Book III.28–29).

As a typical instance he described an encounter which took place in Spoleto between an Arian bishop and the Catholics. On being refused the use of any church "for his heretical rites," the Lombard bishop accompanied by a large crowd tried to take over the Church of St. Paul by force, but he was stricken blind by a ray of light streaming down from above and had to be lead away. "When the Lombards in this region heard what happened, they did not dare to cause any more disturbances among the Catholics" (Book III.29).

The Pope's Letters show that at least four cities in Umbria were without bishops for some time: Perugia, Bevagna, Rieti, and Tadino. The probable causes included the persecution and confusion then prevailing, as well as a lack of competent clergy. The Bishop of Spoleto was instructed to intervene and deal with a scandal involving concubines in Norcia. Dissension among priests was reported in Bevagna and Tadino.

In Assisi conditions were presumably normal and placid, as there is not a single reference to it in the Pope's 800 extant Letters. In fact the only document of the Lombard era which mentions a Bishop of Assisi is a list of prelates attending a Council in Rome in 649: his name was Aquilino. The next appears almost two centuries later: a Bishop Magione at a Council in 821. Then another gap until 963.

After surviving thirty years "amid the swords of the Lombards, "St. Gregory succeeded in arranging a fairly stable peace with the Lombard King, owing in part to the intervention of the Queen, who was Catholic. There is also an unconfirmed report by the Lombard historian Paul the Deacon that one of the Lombard Dukes of Spoleto was inspired to win a battle against the Byzantines at Camerino east of Assisi by a vision of the Early Christian martyr-bishop St. Sabinus, who died near Spoleto.

Many Lombards converted to Catholicism during the seventh century, and the Dukes of Spoleto gradually adopted a policy of alliance with Rome which promoted more harmony between church and state in the entire region. And perhaps in atonement for their ancestors' attacks on monasteries—in 589 they had destroyed Montecassino, as foretold by St. Benedict before he died forty years earlier—the later Dukes founded and enriched several Umbrian monasteries, notably that of San Pietro in Valle, where Duke Faroald II died as a monk in 724.

That important Abbey near the village of Ferentilo in the steep gorge of the Nera River south of Spoleto was flourishing during the lifetime of St. Francis. Probably in the 1190s the walls of its church were decorated with very fine frescoes depicting scenes from Genesis. The Abbey is equally known for its Lombard era religious sculpture. Its marble altar frontal, with primitive ornamental designs and eucharistic symbols, includes a figure of the artist Ursus and an inscription dated 740. This outstanding Abbey is well worth a visit if one is driving between Spoleto and Rieti or Terni, though involving a scenic detour.

Umbria and especially Spoleto are rich in examples of Lombard era sculpture, with its intricate geometric designs resembling fingerprint whirls. There is a striking contrast between the advanced art work of the late Roman era and the primitive, almost childish representation of the human body in Lombard and pre-Romanesque art, as also between the pagan gods' all-too-human behavior and the Christian images of Christ and His Apostles. Right in Assisi this contrast is graphically shown by the Roman sarcophagus of St. Rufinus illustrating the romantic myth of Diana and by a recently discovered eighth-century Christian sarcophagus found under Santa Maria which has a simple cross between plants and foliage made with curving lines like fingerprints.

The dark Lombard and Frankish centuries, roughly from 600 to 900, produced hardly any important surviving church structures in Umbria. Again Assisi offers an almost unique example in the late ninth-century crypt of the original Santa Maria cathedral. We must await the splendid flowering of Romanesque art after 1000 to find noteworthy new churches.

The dominant Germanic Lombard warlords with their characteristic long beards (*Longobardi* in Italian) settled in their own sections of several towns, yet in time adopted some of the manners and outlook of the Italian natives. When they arrived around 568, Latin was still the vernacular language, and they retained it for official use.

With their Teutonic sense of discipline, they provided a relatively secure political administration. In their churches they introduced galleries along the side walls for women. Two major Lombard burial grounds have been found in Umbria and the adjacent Marches. In each, knights were buried with their armor and even horses, and women with their jewels.

After two centuries of domination and adaptation, the Lombard occupiers of Central Italy in turn had to yield power to another foreign people, the Franks, whose rule lasted about a century. However, the Lombards did not depart. Italy in those centuries was in fact a complex racial metlting pot, as Goths, Greeks, Lombards, Franks, and Swabians settled and eventually intermarried among each other and with the Italians.

In the archives of Assisi dating back to the tenth century, Arnaldo Fortini has found significant evidence of the survival of Lombard families and customs. Some of the oldest manuscripts are Lombard legal documents of the years 980, 1000, and 1030. Assisi's municipal library has one of the oldest extant codices of the important *History of the Lombards* by the Lombard writer Paul the Deacon who flourished around 790.

The deeds of 980 and 1000 are especially interesting because both are legal acts of a Lombard practice named *morincaput* or *morgengab* whereby a bridegroom, on the day after the wedding, having ascertained that his bride was a virgin, formally assigned to her one fourth of all his property: houses, lands, vineyards, orchards, forests, streams, as well as servants, serfs, and slaves. The bride of 980 was called Adelberga. The name Itta of the bride in 1000 re-appears in an Assisi document in 1201. The deeds also mention the Lombard royal coins and measures. Everything is regulated "in accordance with our Lombard law." But the signers, though obviously rich landowners, could not write and so signed by marking a cross beside their names.

Fortini sketches a colorful evocation of a Lombard wedding in Assisi in the year 1000, based on these documents, in the opening chapter of his history of Assisi in the Middle Ages (FAME 1-27; cf FNV I/1, 6-9; FNV-E 4).

XIII

Charlemagne in the Valley of Spoleto

The Franks were the first Roman Catholic occupiers of Central Italy, and they were invited by a pope. In the 750s Pope Stephen II made King Pepin the Short the defender of Rome. Pepin then defeated both the Lombards and the Byzantines and conferred their territories between Rome and Ravenna on the papacy, thus creating the States of the Church (including much of Umbria), which endured for eleven centuries, until 1860.

It was Pepin's famous son Charlemagne, Charles the Great, who on being crowned Roman Emperor by Pope Leo III in 800, became one of the major heroic figures of the Middle Ages. His exploits in France, Spain, and Rome are well known. But details and itineraries of his journeys up and down Italy on his four trips to Rome (in 774, 781, 787, and 800) remain relatively obscure, though his presence stirred the popular imagination so deeply that legends and tales created then and later persist in Italian folklore even today, over a thousand years later. We know that Charlemagne made a deep impression on young Francis of Assisi (see below).

Charlemagne must have passed through Umbria several times, so we must survey the little that is related, though largely in legends, about his sieges of Assisi and Perugia. On his first two journeys he seems to have traveled between Florence and Rome without entering Umbria, as also on his way to Rome in 787. But on leaving Rome then he rode to Ravenna, probably along the Via Flaminia. And in 800 he went to be crowned in Rome from Ancona, so he probably crossed the sourthern part of Umbria.

Now it is known that on his way back to Ravenna he was in Spoleto on April 25, 801, when a major earthquake struck Central Italy. Perhaps it was then that he passed by Assisi. A local chronicle places him at Gubbio at this time, which would confirm an itinerary of Spoleto-Assisi-Gubbio between Rome and Ravenna.

Our only source for the reported siege of Assisi by Charlemagne is a late and uncertain one: a chronicle titled *Liber historiarum S. Ecclesiae* written by a Franciscan Frate Elemosina in San Francesco, Assisi, around 1335 (see SISF V, 251, 263). It is a somewhat disorderly and repetitious compilation "extracted from various books and lives of saints and chronicles." Beside legends, it contains some perhaps authentic and otherwise unavailable materials, for instance a version of an interview of St. Francis with the Emperor 'Otto IV (EBB 381), and information about St. Elizabeth of Hungary (CF 35, 166–76) and the church in the Near East.

As to Charlemagne's siege of Assisi, the question of the value of the compiler's sources will probably remain problematical. In any case, for the record, here is Fra Elemosina's vivid narrative (translated from Cristofani's *Storie di Assisi,* pp. 49–50):

> Now we find in ancient documents that the city of Assisi was enclosed by very strong walls and towers and was beautiful with palaces and buildings and was filled with people of high nobility and defended by many warriors. Later the ferocious and terrible race of the Lombards occupied Assisi and inflicted great damage on the nearby territories and rebelled against the authority of the Roman Church. Then the famous Prince Charles, King of the Romans, assembled a great army from various nations, and besieged it

mightily for a long time from the plain and the mountains. Then finally one night some scouts went around the town and found its major drains, and going into them, they observed there a weaker guard and places suitable for entering. And the next night they went in again with a number of armed soldiers and killed the guards and opened the gate of the city. And the army of Charles entered and put the citizens to death by the sword and took booty and treasure, sparing young children. And they destroyed the city's walls and towers and demolished the ramparts and palaces. And thus they made the unhappy city widowed and uninhabited. Then the very merciful Charles had pity on it and had the town restored, and he established in it a new Christian and Catholic people. And so the city was restored, as well as the worship of God in it.

In broad outline the substance of this account is possible and plausible. It could be true of various Umbrian towns during those centuries, namely that they had been prosperous, then occupied and oppressed by the anti-Roman Arian Lombards until liberated by the Franks allied with the papacy.

We can only wonder whether St. Francis knew about this local tradition. It was probably not the case of Assisi's people being very wicked to which he referred in his last Blessing of the city (see Introduction and TJA 18).

Purely legendary stories or epic romances that place Charlemagne and his two famous paladins Roland and Oliver in Umbria appear to have been popular there in the thirteenth and fourteenth centuries. The principal extant text deals with Perugia. It has been condensed in English in W. Heywood's *History of Perugia* (pp. 6–13) and in my *Franciscan Mystic* (p. 5). It tells of a proud pagan Count of Amelia fittingly named Orgoglioso (Proud) who is determined to marry the beautiful daughter of a deceased Count of Perugia. Hoping that he will be killed, she first requires that he defeat and bring there two of Charlemagne's knights. He therefore captures Oliver and another paladin and takes them to Perugia, but before the marriage he dies in a single combat with the famous warrior Roland. Then Charlemagne arrives and converts most of the people of Perugia to Christianity.

The folklore of Assisi also included a tale, still current early in this century, about a one-eyed giant whose food was human gizzards and who was slain by Roland as he was about to kill two monks (even called Franciscans in one wildly anachronistic version).

Just below and west of Assisi there was a bridge and hospital *dei Galli,* of the Gauls, but local historians disagree on the origin of the name and whether it refers to Charlemagne's Franks or to the later French pilgrims on their way to Rome along the Strada Francesca (see EBB 393).

Against this general background we can better appreciate these striking words of St. Francis concerning Charlemagne: "Charles the Emperor, Roland, and Oliver and all the paladins and strong men who were mighty in combat, pursuing the infidels with much sweat and toil even unto death, won a glorious and memorable victory over them, and in the end those holy martyrs died in battle for the faith of Christ" (CA 72. SP 4). This statement proves how deeply Francis was influenced in his youth by the ethical ideals of chivalry and knighthood that were celebrated in the *chansons de geste* and epic literature then so popular. It also helps to clarify his attitude toward martyrdom and the Crusades (see VIII).

Of course Charlemagne did not die as a martyr. But it is a relevant fact that for political motives the famous German Emperor Frederick Barbarossa arranged to have him canonized in 1165 by the antipope Pascal III. And in 1215 St. Francis and all

Europe heard that Barbarossa's grandson Frederick II (who spent a year as a baby in Foligno in 1195—when Francis was fourteen; see EBB 406) had gone to Charlemagne's capital Aachen to be crowned emperor and organize a solemn translation of the remains of "Saint" Charles the Great. However, Pope Innocent III downplayed the role of Charlemagne (cf BSS III, 857). Incidentally Dante shared Francis' view by placing Charlemagne and Roland in Heaven (*Paradiso* 15.139-48).

Information about the condition of the church in Umbria during the Frankish period, roughly 750 to 850, is scarce. Presumably there too it underwent the several reforms introduced by the Carolingian rulers into the church in France and Italy, based on a semitheocratic concept in which bishops served as agents of the king, with civil (lay) enforcement and assignment of tithes among parishes. In 817 King Louis the Pious ordered that all cathedral chapters adopt the common life style and all monasteries the Benedictine Rule. But after the Carolingian Empire disintegrated, Italy succumbed to the darkest century of the Dark Ages, the ninth, which was marked by still more invasions and by the organized disorder known as feudalism.

The successive waves of disasters that swept over Umbria in the five dark centuries between 500 and 1000 were ably summarized in this memorable excerpt from a fourteenth-century Umbrian codex Legend of Blessed Raynaldus, Bishop of Nocera east of Assisi, who died in 1222 (DSPUB 56, 1960, 47):

> After the very great devastation of the Goths, who oppressed the Latins around the year of the Lord 500 for sixteen years, and after the tempest of the Lombards which ravaged Italy and lasted thirty-five years and was checked by Blessed Pope Gregory in the year 590, and finally after the power of the Lombards was

shattered by Charles the Great around the year 800, then the Saracens overran the Valley of Spoleto, killing and driving out people and devastating the land, which turned into forests, and the city of Spoleto and the entire region lay in ruins for a hundred years.

We must now make our way through this "dark night" of the House of God in Umbria and Assisi until a light of grace and reform appears at the far end of the tunnel in the profound renewal that followed the turning-point of the crucial year 1000.

XIV

The Dark Night, 800–1000

The ninth and tenth centuries are the most obscure period in the history of Umbria and Assisi. The scarcity of documents is in itself evidence of the spreading decay and anarchy.

In Rome the shocking decline of the papacy throws a lurid light on the conditions in Central Italy in those worst of all times. As Monsignor Philip Hughes, the British church historian, put it, in the "night of the tenth century... Rome provides the most spectacular of the horrors... the classic 'bad popes'... what they did is truly terrible."

This was indeed an era when God could well have said to one of his saints, as he did later to young Francis in San Damiano, that "My House... is being completely destroyed." And by whom? By those whose calling and duty were to repair and build it up. That process of self-destruction in souls and in the church was never more devastating than in those dark centuries.

No doubt external conditions were also responsible. As if the four great invasions and occupations of the recent centuries had not been sufficiently ruinous, now two more waves of savage marauders wrought still more terror and chaos. And both penetrated into Umbria.

First, through most of the ninth century, the ever expanding forces of Islam repeatedly attacked and plundered the coasts of Italy, establishing an Emirate at Bari in 840–870. Saracen pirates even threatened Rome itself more than once. Pope St. Leo IV (847–855) had strong new walls built around the Vatican and St. Peter's.

Saracen bands invaded the Valley of Spoleto and devastated the cities of Trevi and Foligno in 881. (Over four hundred years later, in 1240/41, Moorish troops of the Emperor Frederick II attacked Assisi twice, but were repulsed through the prayers of St. Clare and her Poor Ladies at San Damiano.) In 883 the Saracens sacked St. Benedict's Abbey of Montecassino and slew its abbot.

But Central Italy's last invaders were perhaps the worst: the hard-riding Magyars from the plains of Hungary. They plundered Gubbio in 917 and Foligno and Trevi in 924; in that year they slaughtered all the inhabitants of Pavia.

Meanwhile, in the 890s, the ambitious Dukes of Spoleto tried to become emperors, but failed. It was not until 962 that Otto I inaugurated a series of strong German emperors who gradually introduced some feudal law and order into Italy and Rome. But the remedy proved almost as deadly as the sickness, for the firm imperial management of church affairs resulted in continual conflict with the turbulent Roman counts and people and evolved into the bitter struggle with the papacy over lay investiture (control of bishoprics) which lasted for two centuries.

Now it is of basic importance for our understanding of the life and spirituality of St. Francis that we acquire a clear view of the major social, economic, and political trends of his times. But the roots of those trends and forces extend right into this period of the Dark Ages before the year 1000.

Feudalism, the dominant social system of those years, was still potent in Umbria in 1200, though under attack from the new middle class in the cities. This conflict actually exploded in Assisi in 1198, when Francis was about sixteen, and the burghers expelled the German count residing in the fortress-castle of La

Rocca dominating the city. Because documents illustrating feudal society in Assisi appear only after 1000, we will treat it below in Chapters XVI and XVII.

At this point we must stress the fact that the causes of the problems of the church in 1200—simony, nepotism, clerical ignorance and immorality, and over-extensive land holdings and wealth of bishops and abbeys—can be traced back to the conditions of the Middle Ages.

At the same time we must also stress the church's innate power of self-reform and renewal which was manifested in the struggle of numerous popes, bishops, and monks during the years 900 to 1200, and which culminated in the renewal or "repairing" of the House of God that was effectively achieved by the two great mendicant reformers of the thirteenth century, Saints Francis and Dominic.

This vast inner reform movement began during the darkest hour before dawn, in the second half of the tenth century. Where? In the heart of the House of God: primarily in two French monasteries, Cluny and Cuxa, the first north of Lyons and the second in the south near Spain and the Mediterranean. And both were to have a profound effect on the church in Umbria.

For from the Abbeys of Cluny and Cuxa issued a fervent revival of monastic prayer, poverty, simplicity, strict observance, and liberality toward the poor which influenced the church throughout Europe and particularly in Italy. Five saintly Abbots of Cluny between 926 and 1156—Odo, Majolus, Odilo, Hugh, and Peter—made numerous journeys to Rome and personally or indirectly reformed a number of important Italian abbeys, including Farfa and Sant'Apollinare in Classe near Ravenna and Pomposa, all three later linked in various ways with Umbria.

It was during his years in Cuxa that St. Romuald first lived the semi-eremitical life and studied in Cassian's writings the spirituality of the Fathers of the Desert, which he then introduced into his many foundations in Central Italy in the years 982–1027. And both streams, Cuxa and Cluny, flowed together in Romuald's biographer, the great hermit of Fonte Avellana near Gubbio, St. Peter Damian (1007–1072), who visited Cluny, admired its Abbot Hugh and its monastic observance, and wrote a Life of the preceding Abbot, St. Odilo.

The fruitful rebirth of contemplative spirituality inspired by Cluny and Cuxa in Saints Romuald and Peter Damian was still relatively vigorous in Umbria around 1200, when Francis inherited and adapted it. We will therefore treat the lives and spirituality and reforms of those two great repairers of God's House in some detail in *Forefathers of St. Francis.*

Of the church in Assisi in the murky and stormy tenth century we know only the names of four bishops. The archives of Assisi contain only four documents dating from the years before 1000, the earliest being of 963. Two of the four concern bishops and throw some light on the church in Assisi at that time.

In 963, Bishop Eremedio, *vir venerabilis,* signed a feudal grant of two pieces of land to John son of Philibert unto the third generation, in return for two *denarii* to be paid at the bishopric each August. Like a feudal lord, the bishop undertook to defend his possession of the land against other feudal lords. The deed stressed that it was also made "by the will and consent of the canons and priests who have been ordained in my holy bishopric," and it bears the signatures of his archdeacon, archpriest, and two priests. According to Fortini, Bishop Eremedio's handwriting suggests that he had a strong, affirmative hand accustomed to wield a weapon as well as to bless. The notary Petrus ends the deed with the customary formula *in Asisi feliciter,* "happily."

Four years later a Bishop Ingizo of Assisi was among the members of a regional council at Ravenna.

In 985 "Leo, the humble Bishop of the Holy Church of Assisi, in your bishopric," exchanged a lot for another owned by a layman and his wife. He is also called Pontifex, and among the witnesses was a judge-notary representing the king (FNV I/1, 28–29; III, 24, 239; FNV–E 23–24).

Thus from the obscurity of those dark centuries there emerges in the first extant documents a clear if limited outline of the basic structure of God's House in Assisi around the year 1000.

The bishops were in a position similar to that of feudal lords. Their staff consisted of half a dozen priests and canons. Their bishopric was the Vescovado or mansion and the original Duomo (cathedral) of Santa Maria on the slope of an abutting hill below the Piazza.

At this time there were no doubt several parishes in Assisi, but documentary evidence of their existence and structure appears only in the following century. The one church building which predates 1000 is the late ninth-century crypt of Santa Maria. The recently restored crypt of the Abbey of San Benedetto (outside the town to the south) is of the tenth century. But the Abbey itself, Santa Maria, and the new cathedral San Rufino, along with all of Assisi's oldest churches, were built during that striking flowering of religious life in the eleventh and twelfth centuries, after the epochal turning-point of the year 1000, when the world did not come to a cataclysmic end.

XV

The Year 1000: Apocalypse or New Dawn?

What a timely subject, daily increasingly timely, from now until the year 2000, is the debated question: As the year 1000 approached, were the peoples of Europe gripped by a widespread fear, even a mass terror, in the belief that the end of the world was just ahead?

In these last two decades of the twentieth century, marking the conclusion of the second millenium of the Christian era, we are now in an exceptionally favorable position to identify with the outlook and emotions of those ancestors of one thousand years ago.

The problem is one of historical fact. Was there actually any such general terror, as claimed by some modern writers?

First, we can well admit that "the times were evil" enough to suggest the imminence of a climax involving Antichrist, Armageddon, and the Last Judgment. Second, since St. Augustine wrote his *City of God,* the so-called Millenium or thousand-year reign of Christ foretold in the Apocalypse (Chap. 20) was thought by many Bible commentators to have begun at Calvary; hence it and the world would be due to end around the year 1000. However, the eschatology of some of the first Fathers placed the inauguration of that millenial reign at the Second Coming of Christ. Another timely puzzle; see TJA 203-206.

Third, the mass terror theory has been uncritically accepted and embellished by a few modern historians following the lead of Jules Michelet in 1833. But in this century scholars have been obliged to discard that sensational scenario as lacking in documentary evidence. The gist of their conclusions is that there was some relatively minor fear or expectation expressed by only a few writers, but definitely no widespread wave of terror. The whole subject has been well treated for the general public by Henri Daniel-Rops in Vol. 2, Chapter 10, "The Tragic Dawn of the Year 1000," of his readable *The Church in the Dark Ages* (New York, 1962). Ferdinand Lot's valuable article provides an encyclopedic digest of the evidence (see Bibliography).

As to Assisi in the year 1000, Arnaldo Fortini had painted a melodramatic sketch of the alleged terror and subsequent relief while treating the marriage deed of January 1000 which we mentioned in Chapter XII (p. 117). But the document itself utterly fails to refer to the crisis.

Nevertheless, the year 1000 seems to have marked another kind of turning-point in the relatively sudden and widespread flourishing of new church buildings in the beautiful simplicity of the Romanesque style. Though a few examples originated in the tenth century, those new churches proliferated across Europe in the "new dawn" of the eleventh. As the monk Ralph Glaber wrote in his Chronicle soon after 1000: "It might be said that the whole world was shaking off the robes of age and putting on a white mantle of churches."

Modern experts on the history of art and architecture in Umbria have noted an apparent "hiatus" before the "almost impassable wall" of the year 1000, with "an impressive flowering of those years of awakening" after 1000 in the construction of churches and monasteries (CSU III, 325, 326, 350).

A significant confirmation of that rebirth right in Umbria appears in this "good news" report in the Chronicle of Frate Elemosina, written in Assisi around 1335, supplementing the "bad news" which we quoted from another Umbrian chronicle at the end of Chapter XIII: God "healed the sores of Italy . . . and made the Latin people be wholly reborn and . . . Italy replenished with men and old cities restored and new ones rebuilt and ancient ruined basilicas renewed." And in the Duchy of Spoleto "the people began to be healthy and multiply, and towns that had been ravaged by the barbarians were restored. . . . The cities of Spoleto, Assisi, Perugia, and Todi were rebuilt on their sites" (SISF v, 263).

The deeper significance of this turning-point or water shed of the year 1000 lies in its relation to the broad subject of eschatology: the ever relevant problem of the portents, prelude, and process of the "end of the world" or "end of the age." The flowering in those centuries of commentaries and art relating to the Book of the Apocalypse (Revelation) proves how popular the subject was at that time, especially in Spain and France (see illustrations in Gilles Quispel's *The Secret Book of Revelation*. New York, 1979).

I have found only one study of the marked eschatological orientation of St. Francis' spirituality: the late Father Cajetan Esser's valuable "Francis, Man of the World To Come" (see Bibliography).

Though the Saint's outlook could not be considered apocalyptic, his figure and function in salvation history took on that aspect among many of his followers when his Order became deeply involved in controversies over the Joachite theories (see TJA 229-30).

And we know that St. Bonaventure wrote of Francis as the prophetic foreunner and model of a future "contemplative church" (see TJA 195-207). So we may venture to hope that St. Francis and his contemplative-active spirituality may yet play a leading role in the renewed church of a new era that looms ahead, in another new dawn after our dark night.

Postscript on Earthquakes in Umbria

Terrified victims of the catastrophic earthquake which struck the area east of Naples on November 23, 1980, ran into the street screaming, "Apocalypse!" And for thousands of them it was indeed the end of their world.

Umbria too is earthquake country. In the 700 years between 1276 and 1979 it has had a total of twenty-four earthquakes, with the highest number, seven, in the Norcia district. Assisi had three: in 1832, 1854, and 1915.

Part Three

Conflicts in Assisi
1000–1200

XVI

The Feudal Lords

Feudalism was dominant in Central Italy for about four centuries, from around 800 to 1200. Two major violent events marked the beginning and the end of this era in the history of Assisi: the capture of the city by the Franks (see Chap. XIII) and the revolt against the German Count Conrad in 1198, with the destruction of the feudal knights' castles.

In this work we are not concerned with social and political history as such, but only with its effects on the local church and with the influence of social conditions and changes on spirituality. We shall therefore supply only a brief sketch of the structure of feudalism in Umbria and then concentrate on what has been aptly described as the feudalization of the church, which can be illustrated by several of Assisi's archival documents of the eleventh century.

Feudalism in Italy was a natural, inevitable outgrowth of the collapse of the Carolingian Kingdom and centralized authority. In this vacuum, power passed to the local feudal lords. Each major or minor lord sought the protection of some more powerful lord in the region, undertaking as his vassal to provide a quota of armed men. Higher lords in turn made land grants or fiefs to their vassals. Major local lords wielded stringent economic power not only over their peasants and serfs, but also by means of heavy highway tolls over trade and traffic through their district.

Thus feudalism was a social system of despotism more or less restricted by contract and custom. Ideally, given a relatively pacific and just ethic among the feudal lords, it ensured a measure of order and social stability, as in fact occurred at times in England. But in Italy the psychology of the local barons and counts, many of whom were of Lombard or Frankish stock, was characterized by belligerence, fierce pride, brutality, and aggressive violence. Italy's feudal lords have been described as predatory, hawk-like, stern, crafty, feuding, and stubborn, addicted to hunting, feasting, and drinking.

The background and symbol of their life style was the basic center of power in those times, not the declining (but soon to revive) towns, but the many fortress-like castles which arose on hilltops and mountain slopes, in strategic locations overlooking plains and crossroads. The county of Assisi numbered more than twenty such castles.

It is no wonder that feudalism was rich in built-in sources of conflict which resulted in minor local battles and wars and in civil warfare within the cities that could be either quarrels between factions or family feuds or class conflicts (middle class versus nobility). It is therefore relevant at this point to list in brief outline the several stages in the evolution of Umbrian society in the eleventh and twelfth centuries, as feudalism declined and was supplanted by an economy based on trade and crafts and money. Thus power passed from the knights in their rural castles to the patrician urban aristocracy and then to the upper middle class of merchants and artisans. The final stage was the rise and dominance of the *comune,* the city-state, which gradually enlisted the allegiance of members of the various classes in a new sense of community and social unity. The process of emancipation from former feudal bonds underlay many of the conflicts, and came to the surface in the two civic accords or pacts of Assisi in 1203 and 1210 (see valuable studies in SISF v).

Assisi's archives supply an exceptionally well documented case history of this social evolution which culminated during the lifetime of St. Francis and must have deeply influenced his outlook in ways which are still to be thoroughly studied and clarified.

XVII

Four Centers of Power

To understand the conflicts of the two centuries before St. Francis, it is helpful to keep in mind a simplified picture of the four most important buildings of Assisi in that period, because they can be taken as symbols of the various parties involved.

First, dominating the city from its steep hilltop, was La Rocca, the fortress-castle, occupied from 1174 to 1198 by a German count as agent of the emperors who strove but failed to restore the crumbling power of the feudal knights. The history of La Rocca before this period is obscure, but it probably served as a stronghold of local barons at least since the era of the Franks. It can be considered a symbol of the Lombard-Frank-German feudal aristocracy residing in numerous castles perched on other hills and along the southern slopes of Mount Subasio.

But Assisi's earliest center of power in the Middle Ages was the first Duomo (cathedral), known as the Casa di Santa Maria, with its adjoining Vescovado, the residence of that foremost ecclesiastical feudal lord, the bishop. It was located inside the lower, southern wall, on a spur of the slope known in Roman times as the Hill of Janus and in medieval times as the Bishop's Hill. Around it clustered the homes of some of Assisi's "first families." We should note that this first cathedral's original name was simply Santa Maria, for only late in the thirteenth century did it begin to be called Santa Maria Maggiore, to distinguish it from the small parish church of Santa Maria Minore (or Parva or delle Rose) in the upper town.

The first major conflict in Assisi after the year 1000 found the city and church divided over the creation of a second cathedral, as if one were not enough for a little town. The division was less between two buildings than between two social groups and their leaders.

This extraordinary and deeply significant contest erupted under the outstanding Bishop Ugo (Ugone), who flourished from 1035 to 1052. We will follow it in some detail in Chapters XIX–XXI; so here we need only state that it marked a rivalry between the bishop as traditional feudal lord and a new class of urban knights who built their townhouses or urban castles, protected by fortified towers resembling miniskyscrapers, around the Church of San Rufino in the upper city, which acquired in a dramatic struggle the original sarcophagus tomb of the Patron Saint, the martyred St. Rufinus, whose remains had been transferred there in past times (on him, see v. 2).

The clerical allies of those knights who succeeded in restricting much of the bishop's power were often members of their own families serving as priors and canons of the new Duomo of San Rufino. In the gradual process of urbanization, these patricians established second homes within the city walls both in the upper town around San Rufino and on the western spur by the Church of San Giacomo di Muro Rotto (near the later Basilica of St. Francis).

But throughout these two centuries, from 1000 to 1200, another center of power developed in Italian towns, that of money and trade, personified in a new class of prosperous and ambitious merchants. Their center in Assisi was the Mercato and Piazza, the main square and marketplace in the center of the city. These middle-class burghers opposed and ultimately vanquished the "reactionary" feudal aristocracy, rural and urban, with its "antiquated" feudal life style and especially its bitterly resented highway tolls.

Tension between these two rival upper classes finally exploded in 1198–1200, when the burghers sacked and destroyed not only La Rocca but many of the knights' urban towers and rural castles, driving their families into exile in Perugia, where they fomented with its noblemen the battle in 1202 in which young Francis was made a prisoner of war.

In addition to these internal, local conflicts between classes, the rising medieval Italian city-states (*comune,* pl. *comuni*) were also divided by the broader struggles between popes and emperors and between major cities and their neighbors, as each growing comune strove to enlarge its territory by making and breaking alliances with others. Thus Perugia and Assisi fought battles intermittently over the five centuries from the eleventh to the fifteenth.

So during the lifetime of St. Francis a fourth major center of power appeared on the Piazza: the new Palazzo del Comune or city hall. Before 1212 it had been located near San Rufino and was known as the Palazzo dei Consoli. That was where the Saint's irate father filed his first legal complaint against his son in 1206. In 1212 the seat of the city government was moved to a more central and neutral site, actually in the former Roman Temple of Minerva facing the Piazza (see III.2). Later, from 1274 to 1305, the handsome Tower was erected adjoining the Temple. And in 1337 a larger Palazzo dei Priori was built to serve as city hall on the opposite side of the square. These successive structures stand as symbols of the growing importance of the comune as the collective community of the city-state.

It was the tragedy of such Italian towns that for complex reasons their leading citizens remained for centuries negatively preoccupied with petty conflicts between factions within the cities (Guelfs versus Ghibellines, respectively pro-papal versus imperial parties originally) or with recurring wars against neighboring towns.

Unfortunately, all too often the church, that is, the popes and would-be-pope cardinals and bishops, became too deeply enmeshed in those partisan political conflicts to serve as a unifying and pacifying force. Finally, in the sixteenth century, direct papal rule brought to Umbria and its adjacent States of the Church an almost stagnant era of peace which lasted from about 1510 to 1860. Symbolic of that rule was the rebuilt La Rocca, restored in 1367 by Cardinal Albornoz and improved by three popes between 1458 and 1538, which served as residence of the papal governors.

It is therefore evident that in 1200 there was in Central Italy a situation made to order for the coming of a great man of God who would bring at least inner peace to countless troubled souls, if not a durable outer peace to society. So it was that St. Francis left to the people of Assisi a fifth center of unifying spiritual power in the immense double-church Basilica of San Francesco and vast Sacro Convento which grateful popes, princes, and peoples began to build in 1228 on the western spur as a lasting symbol of his reconciling and elevating spirituality and message.

No doubt he himself would consider the tiny, humble chapels and dwellings of San Damiano, La Porziuncola, and the Carceri as the true spiritual power centers of his movement, for in their simplicity and prayerful atmosphere lay the core of his method of repairing the "completely destroyed" House of God (see TJA xxxi).

Striking evidence of the unifying and transcending role of the Saint in Assisi's conflicts appears in his dramatic reconciliation of the feuding bishop and mayor in 1225 by means of the lines on mutual forgiving which he added to the Canticle of Brother Sun for that purpose. However, writers who have claimed that he also played a leading role in the social peace pact of 1210 are in error (SISF v,281).

A primary form of Francis' action in bringing his divided fellow-citizens together again has not received the attention which it merits. This was his feat or strategy of captivating psychologically and drafting vocationally into his reform movement many of their sons and daughters and even some parents, from all classes of society but most notably from the then feuding knights and burghers. And he achieved this spiritual reunion not only in Assisi but in many other similarly divided Umbrian and Italian towns, both personally and indirectly through his three Orders.

From Assisi's feudal knightly families, Francis enlisted St. Clare and many of her relatives and friends, including her cousin Brother Rufino, as well as Brother Leonardo, a prominent mature knight. From the burghers he drew Brother Bernardo and several of his first followers. And from the peasants and lower classes came many others, typified by Brother Giles and the imitative Brother Jack.

Though friction between Bishop Guido and the canons of San Rufino was still strong at that time, Francis also succeeded in remaining on friendly terms with both, if not in actually reconciling them. His possible role in the accord which they reached in 1216 should be explored by some scholar.

The only major figure who, as far as we know, was never reconciled by and to the Poverello was that proud and stubborn burgher and greedy merchant, his own father Pietro di Bernardone. In this connection Miss Nesta de Robeck, the distinguished British writer who has lived for many years in Assisi near Santa Chiara, confided to me in a letter she still hoped the archives will one day yield a document showing that father and son were reconciled. . . .

XVIII

Assisi's Lord Bishops

Having surveyed the bitter fruits of the conflicts arising from feudalism in the period 1000–1200, we are now in a position to consider several archival documents which illustrate the process of feudalization and materialization of the church in Assisi at the beginning of that period. It was that process against which St. Francis reacted with his fanatical cult of voluntary religious poverty.

We have no direct evidence of the degree to which the bishops of Assisi shared in the general decadence which afflicted much of the episcopacy in the Dark Ages, which has been described in these frank lines by Monsignor Philip Hughes in his *Popular History of the Catholic Church* (New York, 1959; Image ed., p. 88): "Bishops . . . all too frequently, in these terrible centuries, preyed on the sees of western Europe. They were in ways of life exactly like the brutal, illiterate, and licentious baronage from whom they sprang. Often . . . they married and then made it the main object of their life to transmit the see, like some piece of personal property, to one of their sons. Often . . . they had bought their nomination to the see, and their reign was a long financial torture for the unfortunate subjects, while the prelate endeavoured to recoup his initial expenses."

Here we must stress that those "terrible" conditions in the higher clergy prevailed in the "worst of times," the darkest of the

Dark Ages, around the ninth century. Since that low point, a series of reforms brought improvements, especially the extensive reform movement of Pope St. Gregory VII who reigned from 1073 to 1085. However, we will see in *Forefathers* that St. Peter Damian found just before then in the Marches of Ancona and in Gubbio a number of shockingly unworthy bishops, most of whom he denounced to Rome and saw removed.

The only one of the serious charges mentioned above by Monsignor Hughes that is documented regarding the bishops of Assisi in the eleventh century is one of loving money alleged against Bishop Ugo by some of his opponents. But we will see that Assisi's bishops along with their rivals the canons of San Rufino became inextricably involved in gifts and grants of real estate that made them feudal lords possessing and administering great wealth, including numerous vassals and serfs. It would be interesting to know whether the latter received better treatment from their episcopal lords and overseers.

First, a few words of explanation about our sources, the oldest documents in the cathedral archives of Assisi, because their contents are significant. The striking fact is that nearly all the documents which survived pertain to transactions of real estate: sales, transfers, leases, and donations. These are the archives of San Rufino, and they include a few early deeds from Santa Maria. Perhaps Assisi's medieval bishops kept other church papers, but they have not survived. Actually baptismal records began only after being required by the Council of Trent in the sixteenth century.

What is available has been studied, transcribed, or abstracted by Arnaldo Fortini, and most of it was published (though often in faulty copies) in the thick third volume of his *Nova Vita di San Francesco* (FNV) in 1959. He has aptly described himself as "the poet whom a passion for vanished things had lead to rummage in the dusty solitude of the old cathedral archives" with "nostalgic loyalty" (FAME 1). Those archives are now being edited for a comprehensive and correct new edition.

The first eleventh-century document of interest to us is dated 1018, probably (cf Cristofani 46; FNV III, 334). In it "the humble and venerable Bishop Giorgio," with his episcopal advocate Pietro, reaffirmed his full authority over the Diocese of Assisi as the Emperor Henry II (d. 1024) had so invested him, and the Duke of Spoleto confirmed the bishop's jurisdiction on behalf of the emperor over the diocese and parishes inside and outside the town, with all their lands, vineyards, tithes, and serfs, including certain lands which had been usurped by two feudal lords and their sons.

A year later a new Bishop Guglielmo went down to the first Tomb of St. Rufinus at Costano by the Chiascio River to attend a formal judgment before the local count in a dispute over some land with a feudal lord Pietro son of Romano, in the presence of a royal agent and a number of *boni homines* (then the term not just for leading citizens but for lords and knights). If necessary the bishop's advocate was prepared to engage in a single combat or trial-by-ordeal with the defendant, leaving the judgment to God, with safe-conduct for the winner. However, as often happened, the defendant yielded, and the count re-invested the bishop in possession of the land (FNV III, 333).

According to Fortini, "from these first documents until the end of the twelfth century the bishop . . . came to acquire a vast amount of property, so that by the time of the Saint [Francis], he appeared to be the master or owner (*padrone*) of half of the territory of the Commune" (FNV I/1, 31; FNV-E 26). The church's land holdings were listed item by item in Pope Innocent III's Bull of 1198 (FNV III, 543).

At this point we should explain the normal procedure by which land was conveyed to the church, whether to bishoprics or to abbeys. This process might well be called religious feudalism or the feudalization of the church. To some extent it was based on religious motivation. In essence it involved a gift to the church of land, with or without serfs, often in expiation of serious sins and in expectation of intercessory prayers on the part of the clergy or monks. A more mundane consideration was protection or insurance against the very real threat of appropriation by force by a rival feudal lord.

The religious motivation of the gift is frankly explicit in some of the documents. For instance, one of the early donations of land to the prior and canons of San Rufino in 1029 states that it was made by the two donors "as a remedy for our soul and for that true life where all must rise from death, in order that in that world-to-come Almighty Lord You may deign to reduce our sins and crimes" (FNV III, 243).

In this era of extensive church building, feudal lords with guilty consciences often gave land to the church for the specific purpose that a new church or monastery be erected on it as expiation for their "sins and crimes."

Thus in 1088 Abbot Berard of the great Abbey of Farfa in Latium between Rome and Rieti came to Assisi to accept from Ubertino son of Guittone the lot on the western spur of Subasio where the Church of San Giacomo di Muro Rotto was then erected. In this case the document states openly that Ubertino had killed his godfather and the latter's son "and several others," for which crime he had received from the Bishop of Gubbio a penance of 300 years. The abbot then took over this penance on behalf of his congregation and promised that his priests would pray, chant, fast, offer sacrifices, and distribute alms in the new church for the soul of the donor (FNV III, 262).

In rare cases a wealthy landowner, perhaps a widower, would not only donate to the church all his property but himself as well for the rest of his life, in return for food, lodging, and clothes. In 1193 Giberto son of Bibiolo gave his lands and himself to San

Giacomo, and so did his son Filippo in 1201 (FNV III, 548). These examples shed light on the act of young Francis a few years later in giving himself as an oblate to the little surburban church of San Damiano at the beginning of his conversion; and also on the late vocation to the Order of Friars Minor of the prominent middle-aged knight who became Brother Leonardo (EBB 436).

San Damiano was the scene of two significant feudal-religious deeds in 1030 and 1103. In the first the grantor, again for the good of his and his parents' souls, standing before the altar formally granted freedom to one of his serfs (FNV III, 243). In the second a group of associated urban knights who had acquired the small church donated it to the Prior of San Rufino "with its endowments and books and vestments and ornaments and bells" (FNV III, 86, 357).

Because of an interesting link with St. Francis we must mention here one of the principal and most unpopular officials of the feudal land system, both secular and ecclesiastical: the *castaldus* (or *gastaldus*), originally a local governor under the Dukes of Spoleto, then by extension the overseer or rural majordomo of a lord or bishop or abbot, hence the often domineering and brutal boss of his peasants and serfs; and lastly the constable or policeman of urban governments.

Now it is deeply meaningful that St. Francis often used the striking expression *castaldi Domini*, the Lord's constables, in an obvious spiritual pun (Lord-lord), to refer to demons and devils, our "invisible enemies" (CA 75). Thus after spending a night being attacked by demons in the tower of a cardinal in Rome, he said: "Devils are the *castaldi* of our Lord. For as the *podestà* (mayor) sends his constable to punish someone who has sinned, so does the Lord correct and chastise whomever He loves by means of His constables, that is, by the devils, who are His ministers in this ministry." And he warned those friars who were deviating from his ideal of simplicity and humility: "I put my trust in the constables of the Lord, that God will punish you through them" (CA 92 and 114).

In this connection a dark aspect of ecclesiastical feudalism is the fact that some of the *castaldi* of the great monasteries were *conversi,* laymen who became affiliated to the Order as lay brothers or oblates.

It is now clearly evident that this process of feudalization of the church, this materialization and enrichment, must be seen as a major background factor in St. Francis' radical ideal of extreme voluntary poverty motivated by Christian mystical asceticism for union with God, but also as a sign and protest and example and indirect condemnation of materialism or "destruction" of Christian souls, especially among the leaders of the church.

Here we need only recall his bold statement to the contentious and greedy Bishop Guido of Assisi (see Chap. viii) to the effect that "conflicts and lawsuits arise from . . . possessions, and from this the love of God and of neighbor is often impeded in many ways" (3S 35).

XIX

Two Rival Cathedrals

How in the world did a small town like Assisi come to have two co-existing, rival cathedrals?

This is indeed an extraordinary case, with few parallels. No other city in Umbria provides an example in any way similar. Some had a first cathedral and bishopric, which was later abandoned in favor of a new structure. But it would seem that in no other case did the bishops continue to reside beside the first cathedral at some distance from the new one—a good fifteen-minute walk (uphill too). Moreover, Assisi's second Duomo of San Rufino had no bishop's mansion. Instead it had a *canonica,* the residence of the prior and canons of the cathedral chapter. We may note that the term "double-cathedrals" does not mean two buildings but one dedicated to two Saints, one of whom was usually St. Mary Virgin.

The climax of this tragic division in the basic cell of the church in Assisi took place in a dramatic conflict under Bishop Ugo (Ugone) who appears in archival documents between 1035 and 1052. Fortunately that drama was narrated soon afterward, perhaps in Umbria before 1069, by a thoroughly reliable prelate, the great hermit-mystic reformer and cardinal, St. Peter Damian (d. 1072), in his Sermon No. 36 "On St. Rufinus Martyr" (PL 144. 693–99). His life and spirituality will be treated at length in *Forefathers* because he is one of the most influential of St. Francis' spiritual forefathers.

St. Peter Damian may well have visited Assisi more than once on his frequent journeys between Rome and his Hermitage of the Holy Cross at Fonte Avellana north of Gubbio (see Dante's lines on its site in TJA 219). Or he may have heard the story in Gubbio or in Rome from Ugo himself or his successor or some Umbrian prelate. It has been suggested that he wrote the Sermon while residing at the Priory of San Nicolo northwest of Perugia in 1053.

His vivid account has been accepted by scholars as substantially authentic and hence as one of the most valuable extant documents on the history of Assisi. As it has never been translated into English, we will present generous extracts in this Chapter and the next, omitting the author's scriptural digressions.

After an extended introduction on the honor that should be rendered to the remains and tombs of the Saints, he records in a few lines all that is known about the early history of the body of St. Rufinus. It is significant that the four long columns of the Sermon do not once refer to that martyr as a bishop, nor does a Hymn which the cardinal, who was also a Latin poet, wrote in his honor (PL 145. 953). Yet the Sermon also mentions the biographical *Passio* which was concocted during those years. Evidently the cardinal, despite his predilection for marvels, gave scant credence to that typically "legendary" legend, which repeatedly referred to Rufinus as bishop (though not "of Assisi") and which copied freely from similar legends (see v.2). But he did accept and confirm the local tradition that Rufinus had been an early martyr of Assisi with a definite cult over the centuries.

That local oral tradition placed the site of the martyr's death and burial near the village of Costano beside the Chiascio River, southwest of Santa Maria degli Angeli. As we saw in Chapter XVIII, a trial was held there in 1019. A document of 1038 connects the site with the name of St. Rufinus (FNV III, 333). The ruins of a small church could still be seen there in the seventeenth century.

But in some unspecified century during the "dark age" invasions, the martyr's body was transported into the city of Assisi, as St. Peter Damian wrote: "Later therefore, through fear of pagan attack, the body of the blessed martyr was transported within the city walls from the surroundings of the town of Assisi, where it had been placed in early times. Now the stone vessel in which that body had previously rested was left abandoned outside the walls for a long time. From this, in fact, arose a serious conflict between the people and Ugo who was then bishop of that see."

The root cause of this bitter confrontation was the fact that when the body was moved to Assisi, it was *not* enshrined in the Cathedral of Santa Maria but placed in another church, perhaps built for that purpose in the upper city, on the site of the former Roman Temple of the *Bona Mater,* the Good Mother. Nothing is known about the circumstances of that fateful decision, despite a fourteenth-century legend ascribing the choice, as so often, to stubborn unguided oxen (FAME 48, Brunacci 40).

Now, sometime around 1036, Bishop Ugo decided that his Duomo of Santa Maria must at least have the ancient Roman sarcophagus, the "stone vessel," in which the martyr's body had originally been entombed at Costano and which was still there.

Here is St. Peter Damian's blow-by-blow report of the ensuing struggle over that sarcophagus which traumatically divided the inhabitants of God's House in Assisi:

> For the bishop believed that it should be brought to the Church of St. Mary Ever Virgin, which is the first bishopric of that place, with the plan that, since the mother church did not have the martyr's body, at least it might be compensated by the consolation of his empty tomb.
>
> On the other hand the people declared that there should be no separation between the holy remains and their tomb, and that as the latter seemed to have been determined in a divine way after the triumph of the glorious martyr, it should not be changed now by

human devices. So, arguing thus pro and con, they transported the sarcophagus to the walls of the city, and the partisans of both sides came together at a certain crossroad.

There they strove to convey the sacred vessel—the followers of the bishop to Santa Maria, but the rest of the people to the Basilica of St. Rufinus. As the two sides struggled, a riot broke out, and they went so far as to draw weapons in their anger and confusion, striking blows right and left among themselves. Swords were brandished in close combat, as they raged fiercely and madly, trying to inflict wounds on one another. But, oh, how divine mercy takes pity on human erring and often frustrates our evil wills, so that it even brings good results from bad beginnings! Not a single man was wounded, and not a single tiny drop of blood was shed. And then something even more marvelous followed that marvel.

About sixty of the bishop's followers attempted to drag the sarcophagus to the Church of St. Mary, but despite all their efforts they were not able to budge it from where it was. When at last, overcome by fatigue, they completely abandoned the stone's carriage, a mere seven men of the other group took hold of the vessel and succeeded in conveying it to the Basilica of St. Rufinus with such rapidity that they seemed to have transported not stone but a little bundle of ox's beards!

Then the people shouted aloud, exulting and joyfully expressing thanks to God as their protector, and what God had accomplished together with his people was quickly told by everyone. Then indeed that saying was proved true: *Vox populi, vox Dei*—the voice of the people is the voice of God.

We should note how St. Peter Damian stresses that the party in

Assisi which opposed the bishop was "the people." He uses that term repeatedly without specifying any particular social class or classes. Would that a historian would give us an analysis of this significant puzzle! At this point whom did the bishop represent? Only the rural knighthood? We may find a few clews in the remaining acts of the drama. The next act introduces another striking marvel: a personal (posthumous) message for Bishop Ugo from none other than the long deceased martyr St. Rufinus.

> Certainty in the matter was reached when a certain priest was sent to the bishop by St. Rufinus himself. For as the bishop was not lightly stirred up against those who had opposed him, they were preparing to make amends to him in a worthy way and to appease him by their devout humility.
>
> Then the blessed martyr appeared in a vision to the priest whom we mentioned and said to him: "Go and tell the bishop that if he does not want to offend me, he should not accept any amends at all from the people, but should freely give them the pure grace of his love and his blessing. This happened by my will, that that vessel was conveyed to my church, so that my small body might again be laid in it. Let him also know that if I had not intervened among those rioters and opposed myself to their weapons, a great number of men would have been lying slaughtered."
>
> But when the bishop nevertheless hesitated to accept these words of the priest, behold on that same day a man who had been crippled gladly declared that St. Rufinus had made him straight and that he had been ordered by the blessed martyr to announce to the bishop in detail those very same things which the priest had asserted.
>
> So at last the bishop overcame all his doubts and scruples and without delay did what he had been

commanded, and as requital for their offenses he made a pact of alliance with his people. Moreover that same day two blind men received their sight at the blessed martyr's altar.

St. Peter Damian then described two other major favors granted in answer to prayers which are significant for social implications as both were in favor of oppressed peasants. A cruel man stole an ox and an ax from "a poor little woman," but suddenly repented when he perceived the ax at her feet before the Saint's altar. And a poor farmer whose cattle and sheep had been stolen by a band of twelve thieves, after praying fervently to the Saint, saw all the missing animals run back to their pens.

As a result of these marvels, popular devotion to St. Rufinus spread to the point where it was agreed that his tomb should be enshrined in a church larger than the existing "small basilica." St. Peter Damian continues:

Therefore Ugo the venerable bishop of that see erected a large church from the little basilica in which the holy body had previously been received, and he had it decorated as sumptuously as possible with available funds. Then he had the body of the blessed martyr placed in the sarcophagus which had been the object of the conflict, and he consecrated an altar over it in the presence of a great crowd of people from the entire diocese. Thereafter many blind persons recovered sight, many others were freed from devils, and many released from various sicknesses.

Though Bishop Ugo's new *magna ecclesia* of San Rufino was greatly enlarged a century later, some parts of it can still be seen today: faded mid-eleventh century frescos of the Four Evangelists with Saints Costanzo and Rufinus, and the recently restored crypt where we know that St. Francis used to pray before preaching in the cathedral above (see Chap. XXI).

XX

The Exaltation of St. Rufinus
(early martyr)

The last act in the drama of the birth of Assisi's second cathedral is marked by still more marvels and conflicts. Two major problems remained to be solved somehow: there was still no extant information about St. Rufinus and his life, apart from the oral tradition of his dying as a martyr by being drowned near Costano; and even more vexing, no one knew when to celebrate his annual feast. As St. Peter Damian reported:

> So after those events, no small investigation was undertaken regarding the day on which the martyrdom of the glorious victor of Christ Rufinus should be celebrated. As no historical records were in existence there, they had been satisfied hitherto with celebrating only the yearly solemnity of the church's dedication. However, by divine inspiration a history of the martyrdom was discovered, and the venerable prelate decreed that the feast of the glorious martyr be celebrated on the eleventh of August, as specified in the document.

This *Passio* (published by Monsignor Brunacci) begins with a Prologue in barbaric Latin in which an old man named Maurinus, presumably of Assisi, claimed that he had searched throughout Rome and the surrounding area for biographical

159

data about St. Rufinus in vain and in growing sorrow, until he met a Roman monk named George in a monastery in Anagni of whom he "urgently requested that he compile the life of the Blessed Bishop Rufinus from his records." That is how Assisi at last obtained a life of its patron saint.

This apocryphal fictional biography, filled with anachronisms and borrowings, often calls the Saint a bishop, even before he came to Italy from Asia Minor, but does not state that he was later a or the first Bishop of Assisi. However, an archival document of 1038 referring to Bishop Ugo as a *vicarius* of Rufinus, has been taken as evidence that he was so considered then. Had the *Passio* already been available in 1038? We do not know. In any case, during the eleventh century the martyr came to be revered as the first and greatest of Assisi's early bishops and as its patron saint.

Now it is well known that the people of medieval Italian towns nourished such a fervent cult of their patron saints that they made the latters' annual feast the most exuberantly celebrated holiday of the year. However, the new Feast of St. Rufinus on August 11, only four days before the major Assunta Feast (Assumption) of Santa Maria, the first cathedral, was not introduced into Assisi without a flurry of significant opposition.

> But not a few persons were inflamed with jealous ill-will toward the bishop. And being stirred up and entangled by a spirit of irrational rage, they caused an uproar, claiming that it was a burden for the people to celebrate two feast days for one saint, that it was a superstition to introduce novel, contrived holidays into their regular occupations, and worst of all, that this one had been contrived not out of love for religion but from eagerness for money.

These last words refer to a medieval counterpart of our modern "special collection" on weekday holy days of obligation:

special gifts to the church such as candles or produce. Now just who were these opponents of Bishop Ugo who stand thus accused of being tight-fisted liturgical conservatives? It would seem that they were not the "reactionary" urban feudal lords, because we shall see that they favored the growth of the new cathedral of San Rufino.

The critics of the new holiday were some weavers and farmers who lived on the plain near Bastia, then called Isola Romana (see IV.3). Fortini says of this incident (FAME 60): "It is the conflict between the growing city and the feudal countryside, where the serfs who are under the rule of the lords refuse to celebrate the urban holiday." Here is St. Peter Damian's account of what happened:

> Now especially some stubborn men, who were called *Isolani* from the place where they live, treated that excellent feast day in an irreverent way. With their women-folk they not only brazenly set to work at their weaving, but also freely labored in the fields. But all of a sudden a fire broke out in their houses, and flames that could not be extinguished burned both homes and fields and tools. . . . Finally those unhappy people ran, screaming and shrieking, to the altar of St. Rufinus and begged to be forgiven and promised moreover to make amends for their sins by penance. They were then freed from the affliction of the fire by the prayers of the blessed martyr. . . . So from that time there was no hesitation about celebrating the martyrdom of St. Rufinus, and on that day people came together from everywhere in his church with great devotion.

The last "marvel" of St. Rufinus recorded by St. Peter Damian is significant because it involves Perugia, which was to fight intermittent wars with Assisi for the next four centuries, the first of which occurred about the time when the cardinal was writing.

While a supply of lumber was being collected in the forests on the plain for the new Church of St. Rufinus, some men from Perugia seized it by force and loaded it on a cart, but when the cart came within a mile of Perugia, it could not be moved another inch. Finally the repentant thieves had to take back to Assisi the lumber they had tried to steal from the Saint. Incidentally the vast forest that extended beyond and around the Portiuncula on that plain was called in the time of St. Francis *selva grossa,* the great forest.

It was the destiny of Bishop Ugo to be Assisi's foremost bishop of the eleventh century not only for the key role which he had in the conflict with "the people" over the sarcophagus of St. Rufinus and the enlargement of San Rufino, but also because he was called to serve the Holy See in Rome on the broader stage of church history.

In 1048 he was appointed legate of the people of Rome to the Diet called by the Emperor Henry III to meet in Worms and elect a new pope. Ugo had already attended councils in Rome in 1035 and 1039, when he must have made a strong impression. For he was now given the important assignment of not merely attending the Diet but of conveying the decisive message that Rome's choice for pope was the Alsatian Bishop Bruno of Toul. This tall, blond, vigorous kinsman of the Emperor won the election and became Pope St. Leo IX (1049–1054), whose short reign marked a turning-point in the history of the Church because of the sorely needed and drastic reforms which he set in motion and which were further implemented by his chief counsellor (and later successor), the great Hildebrand, who became Pope St. Gregory VII (1073–1085). A prime supporter and advocate of those reforms was St. Peter Damian (d. 1072).

Accompanied by Hildebrand and Bishop Ugo of Assisi, Bruno-Leo insisted on entering Rome as a humble, barefooted pilgrim.

Unfortunately we have no information about any reforms which Bishop Ugo may have tried to introduce into the church in Assisi, as Leo did in Rome and elsewhere, aimed at eradicating the twin evils which were "destroying" the House of God at that time: simony (buying church offices) and concubinage.

XXI

The Triumph of San Rufino
(second cathedral)

St. Peter Damian's valuable and readable Sermon on St. Rufinus (excerpted and summarized in Chapters XIX and XX) provides a vivid account of the beginning of the process of transfer of power and dominance from the old Cathedral of Santa Maria to the new Duomo of San Rufino, and hence from the bishop himself to the prior and canons of the chapter. After that transfer, the House of God in Assisi remained tragically and traumatically divided.

At that time, the eleventh century, the struggle for power, between the social classes and especially between the feudal nobility and the middle-class burghers and merchants, was not as clear and sharp as it became in the twelfth century. St. Peter Damian's rather cryptic stress on "the people" as favoring the new over the old cathedral tends to give the picture a focus which changed. For San Rufino soon became the stronghold of the urban nobility, the powerful older families, often of Lombard or Frankish descent in part, who moved from their rural castles to imposing new town mansions fortified with tall crenelated towers, as still found in San Gimignano, south of Florence.

The rise of San Rufino to predominance is amply documented in the cathedral archives. As already noted, most of the early documents deal with transactions in real estate, and most are

gifts or feudal grants of land by wealthy and more or less guilty
landowners to the new cathedral. Between the years 1007 and
1099 Fortini found no less than fifty-five, with still more in the
following century.

Just when did this transfer of power come into effect? Probably soon after the triumphant acquisition of the sarcophagus,
with the subsequent flowering of popular cult, as described by
St. Peter Damian. Documentary evidence is unclear. Bishop
Ugo's name appears between 1036 and 1052, but he may have
become bishop before 1036. Already in 1029 two documents
refer to canons in both cathedrals, but after 1035 they describe
San Rufino as *episcopium*.

Here is a striking and significant aspect of this process which
may be rare if not unique. The general feudalization of the
church seems even to have extended a lord-vassal connotation to
the rites of ordination of bishops and priests. The archival
documents of the period 1029 to 1057—more or less Ugo's
term—often stress the fact that ordinations were then occurring
in San Rufino, i.e., not in Santa Maria as in 963. A document of
1045 even states that Ugo himself had been *sacratus* there. And
another in 1052 that he had been *ordinatus* in San Rufino. Numerous references to San Rufino's priors, archpriests, and
priests recall that they too received holy orders there.

This trend culminated under Bishop Clarissimo (1126–1134),
when San Rufino's canons, under the leadership of their outstanding archpriest and prior Rainerio (often mentioned in
documents from 1127 to 1151), became so bold as to claim that
they were empowered to ordain priests independently of the
bishop. Of course the latter only had to appeal to Rome to obtain
a definitive ruling by the Holy See that such an uncanonical
innovation and usurpation would not be tolerated—a decision
which Pope Innocent III reconfirmed in 1198, warning that it
must be observed *irrefragabiliter*, i.e., unbreakably (FNV III, 544).

Thus the canons of San Rufino came to dominate the church in Assisi, in a movement which might almost be compared to the contemporary grasping of political power by barons from kings, as seen in the Magna Carta pact in England in 1215.

Unfortunately we know all too little about the canons of the church in Assisi, apart from the many donation deeds in the archives. They resided in the *canonica,* also called the palace of the lord prior or the house of San Rufino. It was located on the right of the new larger Duomo of Bishop Ugo. It included a dormitory, the prior's chamber, a common room with furnace, a cloister, and a garden.

To some unknown extent, varying through the medieval centuries, like their colleagues in other Italian dioceses, Assisi's canons must have been affected by the various reforms instituted among the cathedral and parish clergy. But I have found no evidence that the important movements for reform of the canonical order in the twelfth century penetrated into Assisi, though they did influence the clergy in other Umbrian towns, such as Perugia, Foligno, Città di Castello, Todi, and most notably Gubbio under its famous Bishop and Patron Saint Ubaldo (d. 1160). In an extensive chapter on him as Umbria's foremost medieval bishop in *Forefathers of St. Francis,* we will describe the common life of the clergy as he organized it among his canons.

It is possible that the forthcoming, much needed studies of Assisi's greatest medieval Bishop Magister Rufinus ii (fl. 1179) will disclose some indication of the condition of his cathedral clergy around the time of the birth of St. Francis. His unpublished Sermons should shed light on that important subject, and we trust that they will be published soon, so that we can treat them in the chapter on him in *Forefathers.*

Now we must briefly outline the history of the successive structures of Assisi's second cathedral San Rufino because for two momentous centuries, from about 1040, when the martyr's original tomb was transferred there, until 1250 and beyond, it was the center of Assisi's religious life and culture. After the body of St. Francis was moved from its temporary tomb in San Giorgio on May 25, 1230, the large new Basilica of San Francesco, completed and consecrated in 1253, assumed that role with a spiritually unifying force which for a while overcame the divisions among the population . . . until later in that century new divisions and rival factions among citizens and clergy resulted in new conflicts that lasted, along with sackings by the old foes from Perugia, until the sixteenth century. That sad and depressing story is told in woe-by-woe and blow-by-blow detail in the second half of Arnaldo Fortini's 625-page *Assisi nel Medio Evo* (FAME).

On the site of a Roman Temple of the Good Mother in the upper city, perhaps around the eighth century, the original "small basilica" was built to enshrine the body—"my small body"—of St. Rufinus. Around 1050 it was replaced by the *magna ecclesia*, the large church erected by Bishop Ugo. And that in turn was rebuilt and enlarged after 1140 by the Umbrian master architect Giovanni da Gubbio (who also rebuilt the first cathedral Santa Maria).

The handsome Romanesque façade of this last—the present—San Rufino was still being completed during the lifetime of St. Francis. The main altar of the new interior was consecrated in 1228 by the latter's friend Pope Gregory ix. And the renovated Duomo itself was blessed by Pope Innocent iv in 1253, the year of St. Clare's death.

Those two great controversialists, Conventual Padre Giuseppe Abate and Arnaldo Fortini, engaged in an interesting dispute regarding the exact location of the new façade and the home of St. Clare. Fortini sought to refute Abate's claim that her family's house was the second rather than the first on the viewer's and the church's left. A complete, critical history of Assisi's two cathedrals remains to be written. However, Gisberto Martelli has given us an excellent study of the restored crypt of San Rufino (CSU III, 327–30).

Its magnificent Romanesque façade has often been praised. We must therefore quote from some of those enthusiastic tributes. "A grandiose structure, among the most celebrated monuments of Romanesque art in Italy . . . a very beautiful specimen of Romanesque architecture . . . one of its purest achievements . . . among the best and most perfect . . . a vision of beauty . . . superb . . . marvelous . . . imposing and austere . . . rugged and homely . . . venerable and picturesque . . . the most majestic piece of architecture in the city . . . full of that severe and sober dignity which is the mark of the Romanesque style . . . extremely interesting . . . rich in symbolic figures . . . the symbolism of the brown stone carvings invites study." Indeed we need such in-depth study. Meanwhile we have detailed descriptions in English in Rowdon's valuable *Companion Guide to Umbria* (London 1969) 140, and in Cruickshank's *The Umbrian Towns* (London 1901) 148–52.

However, the façade of San Rufino which we see today is not exactly what St. Francis saw. Apart from the unfinished art work, in his time it did not have the entire upper or third level, i.e., the large triangular tympanum framing a Gothic arch, which was added only toward the end of the thirteenth century. Therefore the façade which he saw more closely resembled that of the Abbey of San Pietro in Assisi's lower town, which was also rebuilt early in that century.

Incidentally, Franco Prosperi has claimed that a series of small figures sculpted above the main door of San Rufino represent symbolic images from the mystical theology of sacred history of the famous prophet, the Abbot Joachim of Fiore (d. 1202).

San Rufino is of course intimately linked to the lives of St. Francis and St. Clare. Since we know that its rebuilding was proceeding in 1210 and in 1216, he must have actually seen this material "reparation" of God's central House in Assisi advancing year by year.

In 1210 the decisive peace pact between the nobility and the burghers specified that "the consul is to see to it that the work on the new church of San Rufino should go forward" (SISF v, 326. FNV III, 37, 576). In 1216 an important agreement settling a conflict over jurisdiction and income between the contentious Bishop Guido and the canons of San Rufino stated that the latter "petitioned for the assistance owed by him for the expenditures made and to be made in the restoration of the church of San Rufino" (FNV II, 366; III, 593).

Moreover, in 1212 a powerful stimulus *may* have been provided by the discovery of St. Rufinus' neglected sarcophagus in the crypt, followed by dramatic cures, *if* a passage in a controverted fourteenth-century cathedral lectionary can be accepted as evidence, as Fortini does (FVN II, 367; III, 234–37), though some scholars consider it a forgery (see EBB 438). This lectionary also sorely needs a critical study.

Francis and Clare and everyone in Assisi had been baptized in San Rufino, after it became the principal cathedral in the eleventh century. In his youth and during his public career he no doubt often went there to pray and to attend the liturgy, particularly on the annual celebrations of the Patron Saint's feast on August 11.

It is of striking significance that despite the living tradition of rivalry and friction between the bishop and the canons, as proved in their agreement of 1216 (which had to be negotiated by two cardinals, one of whom was Ugolino, later Pope Gregory IX), nevertheless the Poverello, with all the exquisite tact of the saints, somehow succeeded in maintaining friendly relations with both parties. In view of the fact that Bishop Guido from the beginning had encouraged, counseled, and sponsored the young reformer, one might well have expected the prior and canons to have taken a negative stand toward him and his companions. But on several occasions, even in the uncertain early years, they authorized Francis to preach from San Rufino's pulpit. (Perhaps some learned canon reminded them of St. Peter Damian's quotation of *Vox populi, vox Dei.* . . .)

For instance, though we know that the Saint's first sermons were given in San Giorgio (B 15.5), at that same time, when the first few friars were living at Rivo Torto, "St. Francis went to Assisi on a Saturday because he was to preach in the cathedral the next morning. He spent the night there, praying devoutly in a shelter in the garden of the canons, as he customarily did" (B 4.4).

It is possible, even probable that young Clare heard him preach in San Rufino a number of times during the five years before her vocation in 1212, as we can deduce from the fact that she lived within a few yards of the cathedral doors and from these words in her Legend (#5): She "wanted to see and hear him." And it was of course in San Rufino that she attended her last Mass "in the world" on Palm Sunday, March 18, 1212.

Later, probably in 1220/21, St. Francis again went down into the crypt (*confessio*) of San Rufino to pray before humiliating himself before the crowd in the Piazza (CA 39. SP 61).

The popular cult of the martyred Patron St. Rufinus remained fervent in Assisi during the lifetime of St. Francis.

The liturgy of the annual feast day may have quoted from St. Peter Damian's forty-line Latin Hymn describing the martyr's death by drowning, as that Hymn is still sung in the churches of Assisi on that feast in this century (FNV I/1, 64. FNV-E 51. FAME 60, 76). Some excerpts from an eleventh-century Prayer to St. Rufinus which may also have been used are extant; its mournful petitions echo the tribulations of those troubled times: "Remove grief-filled wars. Convert citizens to peace" (FAME 52. Brunacci 27. FNV I/1, 42. FNV-E 37).

Arnaldo Fortini, Assisi's major historian and former mayor, has vividly evoked the colorful medieval rites of the feast's celebrations (FAME 68-70). On the Vigil, under the hot August sun shining on "the mystic poem sculpted in stone" on the majestic façade of San Rufino, with its fantastic animal figures of lions, dragons, and peacocks, the bells in the tall belltower on the left summoned everyone in Assisi to the square before the cathedral for the preliminary offering of candles.

Above the main portal they could see the figure of Christ enthroned between sun and moon, with on one side the Virgin feeding the Child and on the other St. Rufinus. The setting sun slowly turned the pink Subasio stone into rose and pink (on this, see TJA 121-23).

Then, as the bells tolled again for vespers, the municipal officers came forward to offer their candles to the prior and canons wearing dark cloaks and scarlet birettas. The herald announced each donor according to rank and protocol: first the consuls or *podestà* or captain of the people and other civic officials, then the citizens representing the various associations and guilds—merchants, notaries, doctors, and craftsmen in linen, stone, wood, or iron, and lastly the barbers, tailors, butchers, and muleteers. Their large candle offerings differed in number, size, and price.

Only at vespers on the feast day, the next day, did the prior and canons submit their offering on behalf of the entire population: two enormous costly candles decorated with the arms of the commune.

Strange, but this account omits all mention of the most reverend bishop. . . . A rather striking lacuna which reminds us of the deplorable absence of studies of the church in Assisi and of its two outstanding and well documented bishops of St. Francis' own times: Magister Rufinus and Bishop Guido. How long, O Lord, will we still have to wait to know those two very important men well? Those studies are essential for a correct appraisal of the church in Assisi in those all-important years.

(*Postscript.* While I was writing this book, Father Luciano Canonici, the distinguished historian of the Portiuncola (see EBB F248, F249, F29) and of Franciscan Umbria, published a very useful though not exhaustive article, "Guido II d'Assisi, Il Vescovo di San Francesco," in *Studi Francescani,* 77.3-4 (1980) 187-206.)

Visitors to Assisi, rather pilgrims to the House of God in Assisi should not fail to admire in detail San Rufino's splendid façade and within the Duomo to see the medieval baptismal font and the old crypt with the disputed sarcophagus, as also Nicolo l'Alunno da Foligno's charming triptych painting dated 1460, illustrating the martyrdom of St. Rufinus and translation of his body from Costano to Assisi (see illus. in BSS vii, 472). But be prepared for the shock of the Renaissance interior of the cathedral, which was remodeled in Italian opera house style in 1581.

Of direct links with St. Francis, apart from the crypt where he prayed, there is also the tiny Oratorio di San Francesco near the sacristy, the traditional site of the shelter or hut in the canons' garden where he used to pray.

That is the right place in which to meditate on the divine paradox of the Little Poor Man who prayed there for the bishop and the canons and the people of the divided House of God, the "completely destroyed" House of God—and who, by becoming their second Patron Saint, with his reconciling and unifying spirit and movement and Basilica, effectively "repaired" that House, first within himself and then in countless human souls there and throughout Christendom.

That God-inspired and guided process of "reparation" will be further explored in the sequel to this book, *Forefathers of St. Francis,* which will provide biographical sketches of a holy company of monks and hermits and bishops of Umbria during the eleventh and twelfth centuries who were the living spiritual "roots" or historical-religious background of the life and spirituality of St. Francis.

For as powerful reformers of self and others by the indwelling grace of God, they personified that inner transfiguring process of "repairing" by means of contemplative prayer and compassionate action of which the Little Poor Man of Assisi became, by following in their footsteps in following Christ, the master craftsman, the master builder, the master "repairer."

Appendices

Appendix A

Goethe and Assisi and St. Francis

As far as I know, the visit to Assisi of Goethe in 1786 and his surprising lack of interest in St. Francis has not yet been studied, though this link between those two great men merits attention.

No comment would be required if his disinterest were simply a case of an expert on classical antiquity. But Johann Wolfgang von Goethe (1749–1832) was one of the most universal geniuses of all history: poet-dramatist-novelist-artist-humanist-scientist-and-philosopher. How could such a figure of vast culture spend several hours in Assisi and visit only the Temple of Minerva and in his account of that day fail to write more than a passing reference to St. Francis?

This paradox has puzzled and irritated several Franciscan students. Edward Hutton, as an art historian, confessed that it made him "indeed nonplussed and astonished," adding that "it is surely a grave limitation in the culture of Goethe that he found himself unable to" revere both the Minerva and the art of the Basilica of St. Francis.

The key that unlocks this puzzle is to be found in Goethe's frank and readable narrative of his journey to Italy, his *Italienische Reise,* translated as *Letters from Italy* (actually two versions: journal and letters). There he shows clearly that at that period of his life, at the age of thirty-seven, he was obsessed with an intense attraction for classical antiquity, as were many of his cultured contemporaries. Here was "Renaissance man" or rather Neoclassicist man in all his romantic ardor, thirsting for the tangible, sensuous beauty of a pagan civilization.

For years he had longed to travel to Rome. Now, after crossing the Alps, he burned with a feverish haste to reach the Eternal City. He admitted frankly that he tarried only three hours in Florence.

Yet his interest was not exclusively in ancient Rome, but to some degree even in the Rome of the Popes. In fact he hoped to witness a magnificent papal celebration of the Feast of All Saints—but was amazed and frustrated to find that the Italians put on a great show for each local patron saint, but not for All Saints Day. On the morrow he attended the All Souls Mass of the handsome Pope Pius vi (1775-1799), and was scandalized because the Pontiff did not preach a sermon.

We must also note that Goethe, while traveling in Catholic Italy, identified himself as a Lutheran—and showed in his words and life style that he was a very liberal Lutheran. Typical of his general attitude toward some of the all-too-human aspects of the Italian Catholicism of his times was an ironic comment which he wrote after being informed by a captain of the Papal Army with whom he journed in a carriage from Bologna to Perugia that Protestants are free to marry their own sisters and that King Frederick the Great was secretly a Catholic (with the Pope's permission to keep it secret): "I could not but admire the shrewd priests, who sought to parry and distort whatever was likely to enlighten or vary the dark outline of their traditional dogmas."

This background helps us to understand his attitude toward the Basilica of St. Francis which he recorded in his entertaining account of his visit to Assisi on October 26, 1786. Here are some noteworthy excerpts which supplement his enthusiastic description of the Temple of Minerva (quoted in iii.2):

> I left Perugia on a glorious morning, and felt the happiness of being alone once more. The site of the city is beautiful.... These scenes are deeply impressed on my memory. At first the road went down, then into a cheerful valley enclosed on both sides by distant hills. Finally I saw Assisi ahead.... At Madonna del Angelo I left my small carriage and driver, letting him proceed by himself to Foligno, and I climbed up toward Assisi under a strong wind, as I longed to take a walk through this scenery in solitude.
>
> With aversion I passed on my left the enormous substructures of the Babylonian churches piled one upon another, where St. Francis rests, as I thought to myself that in them the heads of the people must be of the same stamp as that of my captain.

Here the sober German philosopher quotes two amusing rules of mental health which his traveling companion had quite seriously given him: "A man ought never to think. Thinking makes you grow old." And: "A man ought never to concentrate on one thing, because then he goes mad. He ought to have a thousand things, a real confusion, in his head." (It would often seem that our modern media have adopted those two formulas.)

"Then I asked a handsome youth the way to Maria della Minerva, and he accompanied me up into the town...." After contemplating the Roman Temple, Goethe walked on from Assisi to Foligno, ten miles:

> It was a very beautiful late afternoon, and I turned to go down the hill... most delighted to be alone again with nature and myself. The road to Foligno was one of the most beautiful and pleasant walks I

ever took. For four full hours I walked beside the
mountain slope, with a richly cultivated valley on my
right.

However, St. Francis did not let his fellow poet leave Assisi
without a little brush with the law and a reproof for not visiting
his Basilica, together with an invitation to return for his feast
day, with the promise of a prayer at his tomb.

Weeks before, in northern Italy, Goethe had been arrested as
an Austrian spy—for sketching a ruined tower. Now as he was
about to leave Assisi, four constables (two armed with rifles)—
again those "constables of the Lord" (see xviii end)—stopped
and rudely interrogated him, asking specifically whether he had
visited that "Babylonian" Basilica and Gran Convento. Goethe
admitted that he had not, but "assured them that I knew the
building from former times, but being an architect I had only
studied Maria di Minerva this time.... They took it very badly
that I had not paid my respects to the Saint, and they expressed
their suspicion that my business was probably smuggling con-
traband."

Offering to go before the mayor, he finally persuaded them
that he was not a smuggler, and they left him. "As these rude
churls moved on, behind them the beautiful Temple of Minerva
once more caught my eye to soothe and console me with its sight,
while on the left I saw the sorry cathedral of St. Francis."

Then one of the unarmed constables returned to tell Goethe
in a friendly way that he had had no doubts about him and had
so told his hot-headed companions, and he suggested that he be
rewarded with the price of a beverage to drink to the foreigner's
health. After he was given more than expected, the officer
begged Goethe to come back to Assisi and not miss the Feast of
St. Francis. He also offered to introduce him, if he wished, to the
prettiest and most respectable ladies in town, as the German was

"a good-looking fellow." Finally, "he took his leave, promising to remember me at vespers before the tomb of the Saint, and to offer up a prayer for my safety throughout my travels." However, Goethe never returned to Assisi. It was not in the design of his destiny that he count a lovely lady of Assisi among his numerous feminine friends.

We should note that his "aversion" was not for St. Francis but for his Basilica's "Babylonian," i.e., totally un-Franciscan pile of stonework. (Incidentally Francis himself used that word "Babylonian." He would call mental or spiritual depression "that Babylonian evil"—see 2C 125; FNV-E 483.)

We might also recall that Goethe was not alone in his "aversion" for the massive structure of the Basilica and Gran Convento. Even the Poverello's companions, Brothers Giles and Leo, expressed their abhorrence for Brother Elias' grandiose plans while it was being built; and later critics have echoed their complaints.

However, as a supposedly open-minded connoisseur of European art and culture, Goethe proved to have a surprising lack of interest for the treasures of medieval art on the walls of the Basilica's Upper and Lower Churches, even though that art was then in a state of deplorable neglect. We can therefore agree with Alexandre Masseron: "We permit ourselves to judge that his exclusivism is a bit narrow.... We understand the enthusiasms of the German traveler much better than his aversions."

But eventually the great genius redeemed himself—though this fact has escaped his critics. As he matured, his interest in medieval Italian art increased. And in a list of outstanding paintings which he planned to examine carefully during a subsequent journey to Italy, he noted (in his *Paralipomena*): "Assisi. In the Church many scenes by Giotto; especially St. Francis receiving the wounds, must be outstanding." Unfortunately Goethe's second and last journey to Italy did not extend beyond Lombardy and Venice.

But what about Goethe's appreciation of St. Francis himself, as man or Saint, quite apart from Assisi and the Basilica? I have read several articles on his attitude toward Catholicism, but none dealing with St. Francis (Kohnen's unavailable). Franciscan Father Ambrose Styra's valuable survey of St. Francis in modern German literature has several instructive pages on Franciscan elements and possible influences in Goethe's works.

I have found in his *Letters from Switzerland* some objective and favorable sketches of intelligent, ascetical, and hard-working Capuchin priests with whom he lodged overnight in the Swiss Alps. He also admired St. Philip Neri and Alessandro Manzoni for qualities which we might term Franciscan.

Most significantly Goethe may actually have given St. Francis a role in the last scene of his masterpiece *Faust,* written during the final years of his life, when he was about eighty. That scene has a cast of characters that includes several Christian saints and mystics as spokesmen for the ultimate wisdom of the elderly philosopher.

They are, besides the Mater Gloriosa and Saints Mary Magdalen and Mary of Egypt, a Doctor Marianus, Pater Profundus, Pater Ecstaticus . . . and a Pater Seraphicus who is identified as St. Francis by some commentators. Did the great poet thus forty years later make amends for having failed "to pay his respects" to the real "Seraphic Father" in Assisi?

The two themes in the last pages of Goethe's *Faust* (Second Part) which have the closest affinity with the spirituality of St. Francis are: first, the contemplative outlook of the holy anchorites with their profound appreciation of the beauty and power of God in nature; and second, their surprisingly non-Protestant veneration of the Blessed Virgin Mary, whom they hail as "Heaven's Queen ... Virgin pure ... Mother honor-throned ... Chosen Queen ... Mater Gloriosa ... Virgin, Mother, Queen, Goddess"! (The last term is of course un-Catholic.)

But Goethe and St. Francis part company in the philosopher's relative disregard for Mary's son Jesus Christ, who was the very center and heart of the life and mind and soul and universe of the Little Poor Man of Assisi.

Lastly, here is a witty, apt, and profound reflection on the subject of this Appendix by my favorite writer on Assisi, Sir William Richmond (see TJA 241–2 and Index), in his splendid book, *Assisi* (Richmond 15–16):

> In the eighteenth century the sham classic was in high fashion, and so hide-bound were its followers, and so chained by prejudice to exercises in proportion, that they turned a blind eye to the real classic with which such temples as the Church of St. Francis is far more in harmony than the Roman columns which represent what is left of the Temple to Minerva. *Faust* is surely an extraordinary human document, so in another way is the story of Francis. It seems strange that the poet who conceived so great a human tragedy should have been content with a view of a few cold Roman stones, when hard by in the Church of St. Francis the touching life of the greatest of Christian saints, recorded by one of the most powerful of all Italian artists, appears to have commanded no interest, not even curiosity, for Goethe, who did not even pay a tourist's visit to the most important shrine of Christian art in Italy.
>
> Fashions influence even great minds. ... Perhaps it is not strange, then, but natural, admitting the pedantic classical outlook upon art and literature which characterized the most intelligent minds of the

eighteenth . . . century, that the Romantic enthusiasm, the fervid effort to reach out towards an
extended ideal, to return to strong emotions partak-
ing of an intense human devotion, which inspired the
renaissance of Christ's teaching in the person of
Francis, made no appeal to a theoretically trained
mind like Goethe's, so scientific and purposeful; and
yet *Faust* surely, as a romantic play, is in nearer kin-
ship with the glorification of pure love and charity, so
essentially the keynote of Francis' teaching, than
much of the literature of the later eighteenth and
early nineteenth centuries.

When I was in Assisi for the first time [in 1868], so
recently by comparison with the visit of Goethe, the
cult of St. Francis had not been started, nor were the
Italian primitive artists regarded with fervour. . . . Yet
I infinitely preferred the living poetry in the architecture of the Upper Church of St. Francis to what
seemed to me the dead archaeology and wearisome
mannerisms of the cold Roman design which Goethe
came to worship.

Now, while taking farewell of Goethe, we may thank him for
his four valuable contributions to this book: his finger-tapping
tribute to Propertius' verses, his admiring description of the
Temple of Minerva, his entertaining report of his visit to Assisi,
and his remarkably acute and critical appraisal of the tiny Temple of the Clitunno (see IV.4).

Appendix B
(see IV, 5&7)
Was St. Francis a "Nature Mystic"?

(reprinted from *Way of St. Francis*, June 1975,
with revisions and a postscript)

At long last we have a comprehensive study of the attitude of St. Francis toward nature and animals that is worthy of the subject, which has been surprisingly neglected, especially by writers in English—and by Franciscans. Our cordial thanks must go to the author, [the late], Edward A. Armstrong, a British naturalist and literary historian, and to the University of California Press for this landmark book: *Saint Francis: Nature Mystic. The Derivation and Significance of the Nature Stories in the Franciscan Legend* (Berkeley, Los Angeles, and London, University of California Press, 1973. 270 pp. $12.00).

Despite several limitations, this is a book which all serious students of St. Francis and nature lovers and saint *aficionados* will relish. Its coverage of the rich material in the fields of hagiography and zoology is masterly. The author, who has written extensively on birds (see the eighteen references in the Index), has also studied divinity at Cambridge and Chinese culture at the University of Hong Kong.

An especially notable feature of his approach is his broad comparative treatment of nature themes in the medieval lives of Irish and Celtic saints which serve as background for the Franciscan legends. I just wish that he had given more attention to the strikingly "Franciscan" Fathers of the Desert, from whom the Irish and Celtic monks imported much of their spirituality. A scholarly survey of the various links and influences of both groups on the Franciscan movement is sorely needed.

Now for those limitations. There are two which I found outstanding. First, a basic assumed principle according to which any incident which has appeared in early literature must be interpreted as a literary borrowing whenever it occurs in later texts. No doubt this copying was widely practiced by some medieval writers. But the factual incident itself could well happen again and again, and therefore in such cases the second and third accounts are authentic reports and not borrowings. The fact that an Irish saint tamed a wolf does not necessarily mean that St. Francis did not. This hypercritical higher criticism suffers from the same defect which the author rightly diagnoses in some later Franciscan literature: it is more redolent of the scholar's study than of outdoor life.

A second limitation lies in the author's sharing in a puzzling lacuna of British Franciscan scholarship, namely the general absence of references to relevant modern materials published in the United States dealing with Franciscan sources and studies, specifically those published by the Franciscan Herald Press. Apparently these American books are not available in British research libraries, for some reason which is difficult to fathom. Yet they are reviewed in the principal European Franciscan historical journals. In the present case this mystifying blindspot is a serious handicap. Somehow the author should have discovered and made some use of some of the score of books and articles on his topic which are listed on page 550 of the Research Bibliography in the 1965 Franciscan Herald Press edition of Englebert's biography.

The Introduction and First Chapter correctly stress that St. Francis was not a pantheistic or "romantic" nature lover, but pre-eminently a Christian nature mystic for whom all creation was a reminder not merely of God but specifically of its Lord Jesus Christ. This is of course a profound and complex subject, but its treatment in this book is admirable.

The author rightly deplores the amazing fact that this crucial aspect of the spirituality of the Saint and especially his practical example of active compassion have been "shamefully neglected" by so many of his followers. Franciscans, lay and religious, still have much to learn from him in this realm which is now so timely and relevant in its close relation to ecology, conservation, pollution, destruction of species and resources, and shortage and maldistribution of food. Here again the challenge of the fasting and voluntarily property-less Little Poor Man of Assisi, with his almost holistic and wholly supernatural appreciation of creation as an icon of the Kingdom, is an opportune subject for our meditation and discipleship.

May the rich data in this welcome book stimulate further study—and action—in spreading and fulfilling the ideals and example of St. Francis in our Christocentric spirituality and ethics, private and social!

Postscript

The late author announced in this book that he was preparing another on *Christian Delight in Nature* treating the broad subject of Christian nature mysticism. I regret to report that his son has informed me that his father died without having completed that new work, but that the manuscript could perhaps be prepared for publication. Let us hope that it will be published.

Meanwhile we are glad to have in this important field Dr. Warren G. Hansen's excellent *St. Francis of Assisi, Patron of the Environment* (Chicago, Franciscan Herald Press, 1970. 75 p.

$4.95), which is a Franciscan approach and a radical solution to the challenge of ecology. In it Professor Lynn White, jr., wisely proposes "Francis of Assisi as a patron saint for ecologists."

And in 1980 Pope John Paul II named St. Francis of Assisi the Patron Saint of Ecology.

Lastly 1981, the 800th Anniversary Year of St. Francis' Birth, saw the happy publication of one of the most brilliant and profound studies ever made of the Canticle of Brother Sun and the nature-mysticism of the Poverello: *St. Francis and the Song of Brotherhood* by British Father Eric Doyle, O.F.M. (New York, Seabury Press. 207 p.).

It gives me intense joy to acclaim this outstanding contribution to Franciscan literature and to praise the Lord for giving us in its author a first-rate learned yet popular writer on St. Francis.

I am preparing a review-article on that remarkable book for *Way of St. Francis* (San Francisco). Here I will only stress this one point which makes it a masterful supplement and extension of the many pages in this book on nature-mysticism and the worship of God for and through His creation which St. Francis lived and taught. In this sense Father Doyle has written a rich and readable commentary on the Canticle which beautifully illustrates the truth and value of Father Gemelli's powerful reaction to the spell of the natural beauty of the Springs of the Clitunno as treated herein. Father Doyle is indeed much like St. Francis: a fervent poet and mystic who prayerfully sings of the unity and brotherhood of all creatures as a call to a new brotherhood of humanity under God in Christ.

Appendix C
A Jewish Ancestry Theory

Alexander Ramati's dramatic account of *The Assisi Underground, The Priests Who Rescued Jews* during the Second World War (New York, 1978) states on p. 31 that Arnaldo Fortini believed in 1944 that Francis was Jewish and planned to write a book about it. But that work has not appeared, before or after his death in 1970.

However, in 1978 his daughter Gemma Fortini brought out a 38-page booklet with the title, *Francesco d'Assisi ebreo?* (Beniamino Crucci Editore, Assisi/Roma). In it she outlined a number of circumstances and conjectures which convinced her that the Saint's parents were Jewish converts. Her reasons include the following: most merchants were then bankers who were Jews; Thomas of Celano's First Life referred to the parents as "among those who are called Christians" and "of a corrupt root" (1C 1); Francis had a predilection for the Tau; a Hebrew verse pattern can be found in his Praises and Canticle. After her work appeared, she learned that the Jews of Ancona had a tradition that the Saint was of Jewish ancestry.

In 1979 a book titled *The Jews in Medieval Assisi 1305–1487* by Ariel Toaff, son of Rome's Grand Rabbi, was published by Casa Editrice Leo Olschki in Florence. It does not treat Francis' ancestors.

We must await thorough analysis and study of this subject. Toaff (p. 4) calls it a "hypothesis . . . still needing convincing proofs."

Appendix D
Needed Studies

Continuing the List of Desiderata, i.e., needed studies of important topics related to the life or spirituality of St. Francis which have not yet been adequately explored, appearing in *True Joy from Assisi* (TJA 247-49), I add here another list of such subjects related to Umbria, Assisi, and St. Francis which I have touched on in this book (as noted in parentheses).

1   Umbria and Assisi

a) A history of the church in Assisi before St. Francis (Introduction)
b) Studies on Assisi's great unknown Bishop Magister Rufinus in 1179, with publication of his Sermons (Intr., XXI; cf TJA 248, d)
c) St. Felician, sources and biography (Chap. VI)
d) Bishop Guido of Assisi, as man, as bishop, and his relations with St. Francis (Chaps. VIII and XXI)
e) Bishop Ugo of Assisi, biography and study of social conflict depicted in St. Peter Damian's Sermon (Chap. XIX)
f) Comprehensive history of Assisi's two cathedrals (Chap. XXI)
g) San Rufino's façade sculptures, with appraisal of Prosperi's theories (Chap. XXI)

h) The fourteenth-century Assisi Duomo Lectionary: authenticity, dating, analysis in relation to the time of St. Francis (Chap. xxi)

2 St. Francis

i) Relations with the people of Perugia (Chap. i.4)
j) His devotion to St. Peter (Chap. ii.1)
k) Relation to the spirituality of the Early Christians, with special regard to nonpossession, as in 3S 35 (Chap. viii)
l) Possible influence on the 1216 accord between Bishop Guido and the clergy of San Rufino (Chap. xvii)
m) Influences of the Desert Fathers on him and the early Franciscans (App B; cf TJA 249, p)
n) His relations with bishops of other towns: Nocera, Gubbio, Terni, Ancona, Imola, etc.
o) The Jewish ancestry theory (App C).

A Note on Basic Research Materials

For students and researchers I want to commend and stress the indispensability of the following research materials on the early history and background of medieval Assisi and Umbria.

The studies appearing in the *Atti* of the first three Convegni di Studi Umbri (CSU), comprising both lectures and discussions (*Verbali*), are of the highest importance and value for the first eleven Christian centuries.

Of the six recent Convegni of the happily revived International Society of Franciscan Studies (SISF), only the fifth deals directly with Assisi's historical past before 1200, but its contents are rich in factual data and analysis. A helpful complement in English is the excellent article on "Francis' Assisi" by Paul V. Riley, Jr.

Monsignor Ansano Fabbi's *Antichità umbre* is an encyclopedic goldmine and handbook of Umbrian history.

Arnaldo Fortini contributed three major literary monuments to the history of Assisi in and before the times of St. Francis (not counting his *La lauda in Assisi* as dealing with later centuries). Unfortunately only the first two chapters (80 of 625 pages) of his *Assisi nel medioevo* (FAME) cover the period before 1200; they provide a popular dramatization of some of the events treated in this book. Fortini's last work, *Francesco d'Assisi e l'Italia del suo tempo*, is largely a revised expansion of previous writings on feudalism, the rise of the *comune* and the merchant-class, with chapters on the knightly and crusader ideals and on goliard minstrel poets and the art of Giotto.

Fortini's *Nova Vita di San Francesco* (1959 enlarged edition) remains a monumental, epochal masterwork, probably the richest collection of documentation on the background and life of St. Francis which will ever be assembled in one *opus*. Its four volumes in five run to a total of 2270 pages. For a general survey and appraisal, see EBB 5. The first two books, the biography itself, fully merited translation soon after they appeared.

Now at last we can welcome with joy a splendid English version: *Francis of Assisi*, ably translated by Mrs. Helen Moak of Philadelphia (New York, Crossroad, 1981. xx, 720 pp. $29.50)—a most timely and fitting contribution to the 800th Anniversary of the Birth of St. Francis. A first perusal of the smoothly readable text and footnotes reminded me of the half-serious claim that Schiller's version of Shakespeare is superior to the original. In several ways this English-language edition is in fact an improvement on the original. The latter's 820 verbose pages have been skillfully condensed to 620. The translator's footnotes supply rich new data, historical and linguistic. The bibliography has been enriched and updated; and the index includes even important medieval Italian terms. The first two chapters provide a lively survey of much of the material in this book. For further evaluation, see my reviews in *The Cord* for May, 1981, and *Way of St. Francis* for June, 1981.

Far from being designed only for scholars, Fortini's life of St. Francis is in the best sense a popular treatment because it is replete with vivid dramatized incidents and semifictionalized characterizations. Its greatest value and contribution lie in the author's unique mastery of local color and authentic Assisi area background. Despite a few minor limitations such as occasional flowery passages and relative neglect of events beyond Assisi, this Moak-Fortini *Francis of Assisi* will long remain a monumental masterwork, indispensable to all serious friends and students of St. Francis. It should of course be available in all large libraries and Franciscan friaries and convents.

Abbreviations

AB	*Analecta Bollandiana*
AF	*Analecta Franciscana.* Quaracchi, 1885–1941. 10 v.
AFH	*Archivum Franciscanum Historicum.* Quaracchi, 1908–.
AP	*L'Anonimo Perugino,* L. di Fonzo, ed. Rome, 1972.
ASS	*Acta Sanctorum* (three editions).
B	S. Bonaventura, *Vita seu Legenda Maior Sancti Francisci.* AF 10.555–652. English tr. in Omn.
BSS	*Bibliotheca Sanctorum.* Rome, 1961–1970. 13 v.
BTA	*Butler's Lives of the Saints.* Herbert Thurston and Donald Attwater, ed. New York, 1962. 4 v.
C	Thomas de Celano. 1C: *Vita Prima.* 2C: *Vita Secunda.* AF 10.1–117, 127–68. English tr. in Omn.
CA	"*Compilatio Assisiensis.*" M. Bigaroni, ed. Assisi Santa Maria degli Angeli, 1975. Formerly known as *Legenda Perusina* or *Legenda antiqua* (Delorme). Engl. tr. in Omn; also condensed by S. Butler, *We Were with St. Francis.* Chicago, 1976.

CF	*Collectanea Franciscana.* Rome, 1931–.
CSU	Convegno di Studi Umbri *Atti.* Perugia, 1964–.
DACL	*Dictionnaire d'archéologie chrétienne et de liturgie*
DHGE	*Dictionnaire d'histoire et de géographie ecclésiastiques*
DS	*Dictionnaire de spiritualité ascétique et mystique.* Paris, 1937–.
DSPUB	Deputazione di storia patria per l'Umbria *Bollettino.* Perugia, 1885–.
EAA	*Enciclopedia dell'arte antica*
EBB	Englebert-Brady-Brown: *Saint Francis of Assisi, A Biography,* by Omer Englebert. Tr. by Eve Marie Cooper; rev. and augm. by Ignatius Brady and Raphael Brown. Chicago, 1965.
EC	*Enciclopedia cattolica*
FAME	Arnaldo Fortini, *Assisi nel Medioevo.*
FNV	———, *Nova Vita di San Francesco.*
FNV-E	———, *Francis of Assisi.* Tr. by Helen Moak.
LF	*The Little Flowers of St. Francis* (I Fioretti). Tr. by Raphael Brown. Garden City, N.Y., 1958.
MF	*Miscellanea Francescana.* Foligno, Rome, 1886–.
NCE	*New Catholic Encyclopedia.* New York, 1967. 15 v.
Omn	*St. Francis of Assisi. Writings and Early Biographies. English Omnibus of the Sources.* Marion Habig, ed. Chicago, 1973; 3d rev. ed., 1977.
PL	Migne's *Patrologia Latina.*
PUU	Perugia. Università degli Studi, *L'Umbria nella storia, nella letteratura, nell'arte.* Bologna, 1954.
R	1R and 2R: First and Second (extant) Rules of St. Francis. In Omn.
SISF	Società internazionale di studi francescani Convegni *Atti.* Assisi, 1974–.
SP	*Speculum perfectiouis. The Mirror of Perfection.* In Omn.
TJA	*True Joy from Assisi,* by Raphael Brown. Chicago, 1979.

Bibliography

General

Umbria and Assisi Church and General History
(see also EBB Bibl. F182–F197)

Adams, Michael, *Umbria*. London, 1964.

Bonnard, F., "Assise," DHGE IV, 1121–1124.

Cappelletti, G., *Le Chiese d'Italia* (Venice 1848) V, 71–121.

Convegno di Studi Umbri *Atti* (CSU):

    CSU 1. *Problemi di storia e archeologia dell'Umbria. Preistoria e protostoria.* Perugia, 1964.

    CSU 2. *Ricerche sull'Umbria tardoantica e preromanica.* Perugia, 1965.

    CSU 3. *Aspetti dell'Umbria dal inizio del secolo VIII alla fine del secolo XI.* Perugia, 1966.

Cristofani, Antonio, *Le storie di Assisi.* 4a ed. Venice, 1959.

Fabbi, Ansano, *Antichità umbre (Natura, storia, arte).* Assisi, 1971.

Fortini, Arnaldo, *Assisi nel medioevo. Leggende, avventure, battaglie.* Rome, 1940. (FAME). Reprinted 1981.

———, *Nova Vita di San Francesco.* Assisi, 1959. 4 v. in 5. English tr. by Helen Moak: *Francis of Assisi.* New York, 1981.

———, *San Francesco e l'Italia del suo tempo.* Rome, 1968.

Gams, Petrus, *Series episcoporum Ecclesiae catholicae.* Leipzig, 1873; Graz, 1957. Umbria: 668–729.

Heywood, William, *A History of Perugia*. London, 1910.

Kehr, P. F., *Regesta pontificum romanorum. Italia pontificia*. Vol. 4: *Umbria*. Berlin, 1909; 1961.

Ughelli, Francesco, *Italia Sacra*. Rome, 1643; 1970. Tom. I.

Umbria and Assisi Description
(see also EBB Bibl. F162–F181, F205–F228)

Brion, Marcel, *L'Ombrie*. Paris, 1956.

Brown, Raphael, TJA 224–45: "Guidebooks."

Cruickshank, J. W. and A. M., *The Umbrian Cities of Italy*. Boston, 1901; New York, 1912.

De Selincourt, Beryl, *Homes of the First Franciscans in Umbria* . . . London, 1905.

Goyau, Georges, "Ombrie." In *Le visage d'Italie*, G. Faure, ed. (Paris 1929; Rome 1924) 161–76.

Harrison, Ada, *Some Umbrian Cities*. London, 1925.

Hawthorne, Nathaniel, *Passages from the French and Italian Notebooks*. Boston, 1883.

Hutton, Edward, *Assisi and Umbria Revisited*. New York, 1954.

Keller, Harald, *Umbria, The Heart of Italy*. New York, 1961.

Meyer, Willi, *Das Herz Italiens. Umbrische Miniaturen*. Bern, 1955.

Raymond, Ernest, *In the Steps of St. Francis*. New York, 1939; Chicago, 1975.

Richmond, Sir William, *Assisi, Impressions of a Century*. London, 1919.

Rowdon, Maurice, *The Companion Guide to Umbria*. London, 1969.

Secret, Jean and F. Durieux, *Assise et les chemins de saint François*. Paris, 1960.

Symonds, Margaret and Lina Duff Gordon, *The Story of Perugia*. London, 1901.

Tarchi, Ugo, *L'arte cristiano-romanica nell'Umbria e nella Sabina*. Milan, 1937.

Tuscano, Pasquale, "Assisi in alcuni scrittori stranieri dell'otto e del novecento." In Assisi, Accademia Properziana del Subasio *Atti*, Ser. VI, n. 1 (Assisi 1978) 95–109.

Tuttitalia, enciclopedia dell'Italia antica e moderna. Umbria. Florence, 1964.

Umbria. A cura di Roberto Abbondanza et al. Milan, 1971.

Umbria. Meravigliosa Italia. Enciclopedia delle regioni. V. Lugani, ed. Milan, 1978.

Vantaggi, R., *L'Umbria.* Narni-Terni, 1978.

Prologue: Umbria Before Christ

(1) The Etruscans

Cristofani, Mauro, *The Etruscans.* New York, 1979.

Hamblin, Dora J., *The Etruscans.* New York, 1975.

Johnstone, Mary A., *The Etruscan Life in Perugia.* Florence, 1964.

Keller, Werner, *The Etruscans.* New York, 1974.

Pallotino, Massimo, "Gli Etruschi in Umbria," PUU 39–54.

Waltari, Mika, *The Etruscan.* New York, 1956. (Fiction)

(2) The Umbri

Devoto, Giacomo, "La città e lo stato degli Umbri," PUU 27–38.

Fabbi, 67–90.

(3) Roman Umbria and Assisi

Bullough, D. A., "La Via Flaminia...," CSU iii, 211–34.

Chioccioni, Pietro, "Assisi romana e la romanitá di San Francesco," *Analecta Tertii Ordinis Regularis Sancti Francisci de Paenitentia* 30 (1962) 649–74.

Pierotti, Adamo, "La romanità di San Francesco," *Studi francescani* 12 (1926) 289–306.

(4) Propertius

The Poems of Propertius. Tr. by Constance Carrier. Bloomington, Ind., 1963.

Assisi. Accademia Properziana. Colloquium Propertianum *Atti.*
   Assisi, 1977.
Fortini, Arnaldo, *Il più ardente poeta d'amore.* Foligno, 1931.
Salvatore, Armando, "La patria di Properzio ed aspetti del
   paesaggio umbro nel tardoantico," CSU III, 379–98.

Interlude: The Clitunno Springs and Temple
(see also Umbria . . . Description above)

De Angelis D'Ossat, Guglielmo, "Classicismo e problematica
   nelle architetture paleocristiane dell'Umbria," CSU II, 286–97;
   cf 62–67, 102, 110.
Du Riche Preller, C. S., "The Ancient Sea and Lake Basins of
   Central Italy," *The Scottish Geographical Magazine* 35 (1919)
   177–90, 221–30.
Eberlein, Harold D., Geoffrey J. Marks, and Frank A. Wallis,
   Down the Tiber and Up to Rome. Philadelphia, 1930.
Fabbi, 218–21.
Frutaz, Amato P., "Il tempietto del Clitunno. . . ." *Rivista di ar-*
   cheologia cristiana 18 (1941) 245–64.
Leclercq, Henri, "Clitunne," DACL III, 1947–1951; cf xv, 1645.
Oliger, Livarius, *Pantanelli presso Orvieto.* Rome, 1932.
Pietrangeli, C., "Clitumnus," "Clitunno, Tempietto del," EAA II,
   723.
Pliny the Younger, *The Letters of Pliny the Younger.* Baltimore,
   1963.
Salmi, Mario, *La basilica di S. Salvatore di Spoleto.* Florence, 1951.
   See 40–44.

(1) Carducci

Carducci, Giosuè, *Edizione nazionale delle opere di Giosuè Carducci.*
   Lettere. Vol. 10. Bologna, 1943.

———, *Carducci. A Selection of His Poems.* Tr. by G. L. Bickersteth. London, New York, 1913.
Biagini, Mario, *Giosuè Carducci.* Milan, 1976; 1971.

(2) Gemelli

Gemelli, Agostino, "Le fonti del Clitunno, paesaggio francescano," *Vita e Pensiero* 28 (1937) 227–30.
———, *Il Francescanesimo.* French tr.: *Le message de saint François au monde moderne.* Paris, 1948.
Sticco, Maria, *Father Gemelli. Notes for the Biography of a Great Man.* Chicago, 1980. Tr. by B. Wylczynski.

Part One: The Early Christians
Chapters V–IX

(1) General

Bovini, Giuseppe, "Sarcofagi tardo-antichi dell'Umbria con figurazioni cristiane," CSU II, 177–200; cf 31–36.
Brunacci, Aldo, "Leggende e culto di San Rufino in Assisi," DSPUB 45 (1948) 5–91.
———, "Rufino, vescovo di Assisi," BSS VII, 466–71.
———, "Santi Umbri nel 'Passionario' di Perugia," CSU III, 243–71; cf 61–64.
———, "Un sermone di S. Pier Damiani e il culto di S. Rufino in Assisi," In *Miscellanea Giulio Belvederi* (Città del Vaticano) 1954/55, 495–505.
Daniel, E. Randolph, "The Desire for Martyrdom: A Leitmotiv of St. Bonaventure," *Franciscan Studies* 32 (1972) 74–87.
———, *The Franciscan Concept of Mission in the High Middle Ages.* Lexington, Ky., 1975. See its Chap. III.
de Gaiffier, Baudouin, "Les légendiers de Spolète," AB 74 (1956) 313–48.

——————, "Saints et légendiers d'Ombrie," CSU ɪɪ, 235–56; cf
    50–55.
Frutaz, Amato Piertro, "Spes e Achilleo vescovi di Spoleto," CSU
    ɪɪ, 351–78; cf 93–96.
Lanzoni, Francesco, *Le diocesi d'Italia dalle origini al principio del
    secolo* vɪɪ *(an. 604). Studio critico.* 2da ed. Faenza, 1927. 2 v. On
    Assisi and St. Rufinus, see 461–79. On him: EC vɪɪ, 900.
Leclercq, Henri, "Italie," DACL vɪɪ, 1694–1700. "Listes épis-
    copales, XI, Italie, 6e Région," DACL ɪx, 1500–1507.
Lucchesi, Giovanni, "Spes, vescovo di Spoleto," BSS xɪ, 1348–
    1349.
Monachino, Vincenzo, "La lettera decretale di Innocenzo ɪ a
    Decenzio, vescovo di Gubbio," CSU ɪɪ, 211–34; cf 41–50.

(2) St. Felician

Acta sanctorum, ad d. 24 Januarii.
Burchi, Pietro, "Feliciano, protovescovo di Forum Flaminii,
    Santo, martire," BSS V, 597–99; cf ɪx, 379.
CSU ɪɪɪ, 223–28.
Faloci Pulignani, Michele, "San Francesco e la città di Foligno,"
    MF 6 (1895) 3–15.
Lanzoni, 446–53.
"Vita S. Feliciani martyris episcopi fulginatis," AB 9 (1890)
    379–92.

Part Two: The Dark Ages
Chapters x–xv

(1) St. Gregory The Great

Giunta, Francesco, "I Goti e l'Umbria," CSU ɪɪ, 201–09; cf
    37–41.
Gregory the Great, St., *The Dialogues of St. Gregory the Great.* Tr.
    by R. Deferrari. New York, 1959.

Petrocchi, Massimo, "Su alcuni atti di governo ecclesiastico di san Gregorio Magno inerenti alle diocesi di Umbria, Tuscia e Sabina," CSU ii, 343–50.

(2) Charlemagne

Catalano, Michele, "La leggenda cavalleresca in Assisi," *Archivum Romanicum* 8 (1924) 452–58.
———, "Il romanzo di Perugia e Corciano," DSPUB 27 (1924) 41–151.
Fossier, F., "Les chroniques de fra Paolo da Gualdo et de fra Elemosina . . .," *Mélanges de l'Ecole française de Rome* 89.1 (1977) 411–83.
Heywood, William, *A History of Perugia* (London 1910) 6–13.
Hodgkin, Thomas, *Italy and Her Invaders*. Oxford, 1885–1899. 8 v. in 9. See v. 6–8.

(3) The Year 1000

Daniel-Rops, Henri, *The Church in the Dark Ages*. New York, 1960–1962. 2 v.
Esser, Cajetan, "Francis, Man of the World To Come," in his *Repair My House* (Chicago 1963) 15–45.
FAME 1–6, 24–25.
Focillon, Henri, *The Year 1000*. New York, 1969.
Lot, Ferdinand, "Le mythe des terreurs de l'an mille," *Mercure de France* 301 (1947) 639–55.

Part Three: Conflicts in Assisi
Chapters XVI–XXI

(1) General

Blanshei, Sarah R., *Perugia, 1260–1340. Conflict and Change in a Medieval Italian Urban Society*. Philadelphia, 1976. Also relevant for twelfth century.

Fortini, Arnaldo, *Francesco d'Assisi e l'Italia del suo tempo.* Rome, 1968.

———, FNV iii, 7–227: "Assisi al tempo del Santo." See also I/1, 5–52: "Signori e servi; I/1, 55–102: "La città dei guerrieri e dei mercanti"; I/2, 131–219: "Le fazioni e la guerra di Perugia." In English tr., see *Francis of Assisi,* FNV-E 1–84, 119–65.

Le Goff, J., "Le vocabulaire des catégories sociales chez s. François d'Assise et ses biographes du xiiie siècle," In *Ordres et classes. Colloque d'histoire sociale . . . 1967* (Paris 1973) 93–123.

Mochi Onory, Sergio, *Ricerche sui poteri civili dei vescovi nelle città umbre durante l'alto medioevo.* Rome, 1930.

Riley, Paul V., Jr., "Francis' Assisi: Its Political and Social History, 1175–1225," *Franciscan Studies* 34 (1974) 393–424.

Roggen, Heribert, "Die Lebensform des hl. Franziskus von Assisi in ihrem Verhältnis zur feudalen und bürgerlichen Gesellschaft Italiens," *Franziskanische Studien* 46 (1964) 1–54, 287–321.

Schmucki, Oktavian, "Assisi civitas tempore Sancti Francisci," CF 49.3/4 (1979) 277–89.

Società internazionale di Studi Francescani. *Assisi al tempo di San Francesco.* Atti del v Convegno. Assisi, 1978. Contains eight important studies; especially relevant for this book: Attilio Bartoli Langeli, "La realtà sociale assisana e il patto del 1210," 271–336.

Vescovi e diocesi in Italia nel Medioevo (*Sec.* ix–xiii). Atti del ii Convegno di storia della Chiesa in Italia, Roma, 1961. Padua, 1964.

(2) San Rufino Cathedral

Abate, Giuseppe, "Nuovi studi sull'ubicazione della Casa paterna di S. Chiara d'Assisi," DSPUB 50 (1953) 1–37.

Brunacci, Aldo, "Note storiche sulla Chiesa cattedrale di San Rufino in Assisi," *Annuario del Liceo Classico Properzio* (Assisi) 1951/52, 207–16.

Cardelli, Enrico, *Studio costruttivo della Chiesa di San Rufino in Assisi.* Rome, 1929.

_____, *Tentativo di ripristino ideale della Chiesa di San Rufino in Assisi.* Assisi, 1969.

Fortini, Arnaldo, "La casa paterna di Santa Chiara," FNV ii, 351-82 (from AFH 48 (1955) 160-94).

_____, "Sull'epoca in cui fu costruita la primitiva Chiesa di S. Rufino in Assisi," *Italia francescana* 30 (1955) 352-58.

Martelli, Gisberto, "Le più antiche cripte dell'Umbria," CSU iii, 323-53; see 326-30 and pl. 39-40.

Peter Damian, St., *Carmina et Preces.* cxii. De S. Ruffino martyre. Hymnus. PL 145, 953-54.

_____, Sermo xxxvi. De Sancto Ruffino martyre. PL 144, 693-54.

Prosperi, Franco, *La facciata della cattedrale di Assisi. La mistica gioachimita prefrancescana nella simbologia delle sculture.* Perugia, 1968.

Appendix A: Goethe

Goethe, Johann Wolfgang von, *Werke* (Weimar and various editions): *Italienische Reise; Tagebuch der italienische Reise; Paralipomena.*

_____, *Letters from Italy,* in *The Works of Goethe.* London and New York, 1902. vol. 3. Also (but omitting Assisi): *Italian Journey,* London, 1962. *From Lake Garda to Sicily.* London, 1968.

Hohendorf, Horst, *The Life and Times of Goethe.* London, 1967. (Portraits of Greatness)

Kohnen, Mansueto, "Goethe e Francisco de Asis," *Verbum* (Rio de Janeiro) 6 (1949) 276-84.

Meinhold, Peter, "Goethes Begegnung mit dem Katholicismus in Italien," *Saeculum* 2 (1951) 173-224.

Styra, Ambros, *Franziskus von Assisi in der neuerem deutschen Literatur.* Breslau, 1928.

Zarlo, Antonio, "Goethe e il cattolicismo," *Nuova Antologia* 3 ser., 43 (1893) 673-89.

Index

This index of names and persons and places is not exhaustive. It omits some non-Franciscan items, as well as "Assisi" and "Umbria."

Churches are listed under their names, e.g. "San Salvatore (Spoleto)," "San Salvatore (Terni)."

Bishops of Assisi are entered under their names and in an alphabetical list with dates under "Bishops of Assisi."

Fifty items related to the life, personality, or spirituality of St. Francis are listed under "Francis of Assisi and . . ."

Subject sections of the Bibliography (but not authors) have been included.

CATHEDRAL OF SAN RUFINO IN ASSISI

The majestic Romanesque façade of Assisi's San Rufino Duomo (cathedral) was completed during the lifetime of St. Francis. The new main altar was consecrated in 1228. The triangular upper level was added later in that century. The façade is rich in symbolic sculptured figures and has been called one of "the best and most perfect monuments of Romanesque art in Italy, imposing and austere, severe and sober, a vision of beauty." (See XXI.) —Franciscan Herald Press photo.

THE ROMAN TEMPLE OF MINERVA IN ASSISI
Built under the Emperor Augustus (31 B.C. - 14 A.D.) on Assisi's Piazza, with six Corinthian columns, the Temple of Minerva became the town hall in 1212 and in 1539 the Church of Santa Maria sopra Minerva. It was admired and praised by Goethe in 1786. (See III.2 and Appendix A.) —Franciscan Herald Press photo.

THE SPRINGS AND PARK OF THE CLITUNNO
Beside the highway between Foligno and Spoleto, the Springs of the Clitunno River became a famous shrine of the river-god Clitumnus in Roman times, amply described by Pliny the Younger and praised by poets from Virgil to Byron and Carducci. This paradise-like park was aptly called a "Franciscan landscape" by Father Agostino Gemelli, O.F.M. (See IV.) —Franciscan Herald Press photo.

FLOWERING CROSS ON CLITUNNO TEMPLE
Sculpted Early Christian symbolic flowering Cross on the pediment of the Clitunno Temple, adorned with leaves amid vine tendrils and clusters of grapes, an outstanding example of Early Christian symbolism in art. (See IV.4.) —Tarchi photo.

THE EARLY CHRISTIAN TEMPLE OF THE CLITUNNO
Originally erected near the Springs of the Clitunno perhaps as a late classical temple around the year 400 A.D., then completed as one of Umbria's first Christian churches in the fifth or sixth or seventh century with some of the oldest Christian paintings in Umbria, this small Temple has been termed "tiny, elegant, sober, and rustic," with a "Franciscan" simplicity and beauty. According to a local oral tradition, the first Christians of the Valley of Spoleto used it as a regional baptismal shrine. (See IV.4.) —Tarchi photo.

THE CHURCH OF SAN PIETRO OUTSIDE SPOLETO
The Church of San Pietro outside Spoleto was founded in the fifth century by Bishop
Achilleus, then enlarged in the twelfth century, when skilled artists sculpted on the new
façade a remarkable set of animal figures and symbols, one of the masterpieces of
medieval art in Umbria. (See IX.2.) —Tarchi photo.

MAP 3 ITALY

Grand St. Bernard
Mont Cenis
Novara
PIEMONTE
Allesandria
Pavia
LOMBARDY
Milan
Bergamo
Brescia
TRENTINO
Trent
VENETO
Verona
Vicenza
Padua
Venice
Islet near Burno
S. Francesco del Deserto

LIGURIA
Genoa
Pontremoli
Piacenza
Parma
Modena
Bologna
Imola
EMILIA
PO RIVER
VIA EMILIA

Lucca
Pisa
Livorno
Fucecchio
ARNO RIVER
Florence
Faenza
Forli
Cesena
Bagno
Rimini
San Marino
San Leo
Fano
La Verna
San Sepolcro
Urbino
TUSCANY
Siena
Arezzo
Cagli
Ancona
Chiana Swamps
Gubbio
Perugia
MARCHE
VIA AURELIA
Chiusi
Assisi
VIA E. TRASIMENE
Orvieto
UMBRIA
Nocera
Foligno
Fermo
LAKE DI BOLSENA
Codi
Duchy of Spoleto
Viterbo
Orte
Cepni
SALERIA
Marni
Rieti
CASSIA DI FRANCIGENA
Rome
Tagliacozza
Penni
Chieti
Bellegra
Subiaco
Celano
Monte Gargano
Sulmona
CORSICA
LAZIO
Sora
ABRUZZI
Ceprano
Monte Cassino
Foggia
Gaeta
CALORE RIVER
CAMPANIA
PUGLIA
Naples
Avellino
Bari
SARDINIA
OFANO RIVER
BASILICATA
Brindi
TYRRHENIAN
SEA
ADRIATIC SEA
CALABRIA
SICILY

© 1965, Franciscan Herald Press